Family and Succession Law in Germai

C000122299

Family and Succession Law in Germany

by

Peter Gottwald
Dieter Schwab
and
Eva Büttner

This book was originally published as a monograph in the International Encyclopaedia of Laws/Family and Succession Law

2001

Kluwer Law International
The Hague – London – Boston

Published by:
Kluwer Law International
P.O. Box 85889, 2508 CN The Hague, The Netherlands
sales@kli.wkap.nl
http://www.kluwerlaw.com

Sold and Distributed in North, Central and South America by:
Kluwer Law International
101 Philip Drive, Norwell, MA 02061, USA
kluwerlaw@wkap.com

Sold and Distributed in all other countries by:
Kluwer Law International
Distribution Centre, P.O. Box 322, 3300 AH Dordrecht, The Netherlands

A C.I.P. Catalogue record for this book is available from the Library of Congress

Printed on acid-free paper

Cover design: The Bears Communications, Amsterdam

ISBN 90 411 1632 X

© 2001 Kluwer Law International

Kluwer Law International incorporates the publishing programmes of Graham & Trotman Ltd., Kluwer Law and Taxation Publishers and Martinus Nijhoff Publishers.

This publication is protected by international copyright law.
All rights reserved. No part of this publication may be reproduced, stored in a retrieval system, or transmitted in any form or by any means, electronic, mechanical, photocopying, recording or otherwise, without the prior permission of the publisher.

The Authors

Dieter Schwab (born 1935) is Professor at the Faculty of Law of the University of Regensburg (Germany). He teaches civil law including family law and legal history.

Curriculum vitae: study of law at the universities of Munich and Würzburg 1954–1958, graduated Dr. jur. utr., Würzburg, 1960. Habilitation (Ruhr-Universität Bochum) 1966. Since 1968 Chair of Civil Law and German Legal History, Universität Gießen. In 1974 accepted a call to the Chair of Civil Law and German Legal History at the University of Regensburg. Chairman of the Family Law Association (Wissenschaftliche Vereinigung für Familienrecht) 1987–1999; Member of the International Society of Family Law, the Deutscher Familiengerichtstag and numerous international associations.

Publications (extract): *Grundlagen und Gestalt der staatlichen Ehegesetzgebung in der Neuzeit* (1967), *Einführung in das Zivilrecht* (1974, 14th ed. 2000); *Familienrecht* (1980, 10th ed. 1999); *Handbuch des Scheidungsrechts* (1977; 4th ed. 2000); *Kommentierung des Vormundschafts-, Betreuungs- und Pflegschaftsrecht im Münchener Kommentar* (since 2nd ed.); *Geschichtliches Recht und moderne Zeiten. Ausgewählte Rechtshistorische Aufsätze*, hg. von Diethelm Klippel (1995); *Meine Rechte bei Trennung und Scheidung* (dtv-Taschenbuch, together with Bernhard Töpper), 3rd ed. 1998. Joint editor-in-chief FamRZ (Family Law Journal), co-editor 'Beiträge zum europäischen Familienrecht' and 'FamRZ-Bücher', co-editor 'Rechtshistorischen Reihe'.

Peter Gottwald

1944	Born in Breslau (now Wroclaw).
1963–1967	Studies of Law at University of Munich and Free University of Berlin.
1968 and 1971	First and Second State Exam in Law, Munich.
1969 – 1977	Research Assistant, University of Munich and University of Erlangen (with Professor Karl Heinz Schwab).
1974	Graduation as Dr. jur. utr.

The Authors

1977   Graduation as Dr. jur. habil. (habilitation) and appointment as Full Professor, University of Bayreuth, chair of Civil Law and Civil Procedure.

1983   Appointment to the chair of Civil Law, Procedural Law and Conflict of Laws, University of Regensburg.

1981–1989   Simultaneously Part-time Judge, Regional Court of Appeal, Bamberg, and Regional Court of Appeal, Munich.

Calls to the Free University of Berlin, the University of Erlangen, the University of Tübingen and the University of Zürich/Switzerland. Editor-in-chief and Managing editor, Journal of Family Law ('FamRZ')(since 1987). Secretary General, International Association of Procedural Law (since 1995). President of the (German) Association of International Procedural Law (since 1997).

Most important publications: *Münchener Kommentar zum BGB* (1st to 3rd edition 1981/94: §§328–335; 3rd edition 1994: §§315–319, 336–345); *Münchener Kommentar zur ZPO* (1st and 2nd edition 1992/2000: §§322–328, 722–723; treaties of International Civil Procedural Law); *Insolvenzrechts-Handbuch* (1st and 2nd edition 1990/2000); Rosenberg/Schwab/Gottwald, *Zivilprozessrecht*, 15th edition 1993; Nagel/Gottwald, *Internationales Zivilprozessrecht*, 4th edition 1997; *Internationale Schiedsgerichtsbarkeit* (International Arbitration), 1997; *Sachenrecht* (case book) (10th to 16th edition 1980/98); *Prozessformularbuch Familienrecht*, 2001.

Eva Büttner (born 1971) is a Research Assistant at the University of Regensburg and a trainee lawyer with the Higher Regional Court at Nürnberg.

Curriculum vitae: study of law at the universities of Bonn, Lausanne, Singapore and Regensburg (1990–1995). Magister in European and Comparative Law, University of Oxford (1996), research for doctoral thesis, Oxford, 1996–1997. Since 1998 Referendariat, Higher Regional Court, Nürnberg.

Publications (extract): 'Die Stellung des nichtehelichen Kindes im preußischen Allgemeinen Landrecht', FamRZ 1994, 1495; 'Kindschaftsrechtsreform in England – ein Vergleich mit den deutschen Reformplänen', FamRZ 1997, 895.

Table of Contents

Table of Contents

Table of Contents

Table of Contents

Table of Contents

Table of Contents

Chapter 3. The Legal Position of the Beneficiary 145

Table of Contents

List of Abbreviations

AG	Amtsgericht (County Court)
Art.	Article
BGB	Bürgerliches Gesetzbuch (Civil Code)
BGBl.	Bundesgesetzblatt (Federal Law Gazette)
BGH	Bundesgerichtshof (Federal Court of Justice)
BGHZ	Entscheidungen des Bundesgerichtshofs in Zivilsachen (official Collection of civil law decisions of the Federal Court of Justice)
BSHG	Bundessozialhilfegesetz (Federal Social Assistance Act)
BtG	Gesetz zur Reform des Rechts der Vormundschaft und Pflegschaft für Volljährige (Betreuungsgesetz) (Care and Control Act)
BVerfG	Bundesverfassungsgericht (Federal Constitutional Court)
BVerfGE	Entscheidungen des Bundesverfassungsgerichts (official collection of decisions of the Federal Constitutional Court)
cf.	compare with
ed.	edition/editor
e.g.	for example
EheG	Ehegesetz (Marriage Act)
EheschlRG	Eheschließungsrechtsgesetz (Formation of Marriages Act)
1. EheRG	Erstes Gesetz zur Reform des Ehe- und Familienrechts (First Reform Law on Marriage and the Family)
EinigV	Einigungsvertrag (Treaty on German Reunification)
etc.	*et cetera*
FamRZ	Zeitschrift für das gesamte Familienrecht (Journal of Common Family Law)
FGB	Familiengesetzbuch (Family Law Code, GDR)
FGG	Gesetz über die Angelegenheiten der freiwilligen Gerichtsbarkeit (Judicature Act for non-contentious matters)
GG	Grundgesetz (Basic Law)
GVG	Gerichtsverfassungsgesetz (Judicature Act)
HausratsVO	Hausratsverordnung (Regulation on Household Effects)
HGB	Handelsgesetzbuch (Commercial Code)
i.e.	*id est*
JGG	Jugendgerichtsgesetz (Juvenile Courts Act)
KindRG	Kindschaftsrechtsreformgesetz (Child Law Reform Act)
KindUG	Kindesunterhaltsgesetz (Child Support Act)

List of Abbreviations

LG	Landgericht (Regional Court)
NamÄndG	Namensänderungsgesetz (Law on the change of names)
NJW	Neue Juristische Wochenschrift (The New Juristic Weekly Journal)
No.	number
OLG	Oberlandesgericht (Higher Regional Court)
p.	page
PStG	Personenstandsgesetz (Act on Civil Status)
SGB	Sozialgesetzbuch (Code of Social Law)
StGB	Strafgesetzbuch (Penal Code)
sq./ sqq.	following page/s or paragraph/s
VerschG	Verschollenheitsgesetz (Law on Missing Persons)
vol.	volume
VormG	Vormundschaftsgericht (Guardianship Court)
ZGB	Zivilgesetzbuch (Civil Code, GDR)
ZPO	Zivilprozeßordnung (Civil Procedure Act)

General Introduction

§1. General Background of the Country (Demographic Data)

1. The Federal Republic of Germany is a parliamentary democracy situated in the heart of Europe. Since the reunification of 1990 the Federation consists of sixteen Member States ('Länder'): Baden-Württemberg, Bayern, Berlin, Brandenburg, Bremen, Hamburg, Hessen, Mecklenburg-Vorpommern, Niedersachsen, Nordrhein-Westfalen, Rheinland-Pfalz, Saarland, Sachsen, Sachsen-Anhalt, Schleswig-Holstein and Thüringen.

2. The chief executive is the Federal Chancellor, who is elected by the country's legislature, the Bundestag. The second legislative chamber is the assembly of the states (Bundesrat). The states have their own sovereignty, elected parliament, government and independent judiciary. They enjoy considerable law-making powers, primarily in the fields of culture, education and internal security and they represent the main administrative body for the execution of both state and federal laws.

3. Germany covers an area of about 357,000 square kilometres. At the end of 1997, the country had a population of about 82.0 million (including 7.3 million foreigners) – the largest in Europe after the Russian Federation. The population is distributed rather unevenly, densely populated regions as the Rhine-Ruhr industrial area or the Rhine-Main area around Frankfurt contrast with thinly populated areas as the heathlands of the North German Plain or the Bavarian Forest. Nearly one third of the population (about 26 million people) live in the 84 large cities with more than 100,000 inhabitants. Of the 82.0 million inhabitants, around 40 million are male and 42 million are female.

4. Since the 1970s, the population in both the old and new states has been in decline. Whereas in 1950 around 1,117,000 children were born, in 1998 this number had shrunk to 782,000. These figures represent one of the lowest birth-rates in the world and in view of the demographic development of the country, they are alarming: In 1998, e.g., the number of deaths exceeded the number of births by 6,900. Likewise, the number of marriages has deceased significantly since the middle of the 20th century (1950: 750,452 – 1997: 422,776 – 1998: 417,000). Divorces have multiplied in the same time-span, with a new high of 192,438 divorces per year in

1998. At the same time, the number of couples living in cohabitation outside marriage has risen from 340,000 in 1978 to 1,982,000 in 1998.

§2. HISTORICAL BACKGROUND OF FAMILY AND SUCCESSION LAW

5. In the past centuries family law in Germany has been strongly influenced by the Christian churches. During the middle ages the Catholic Church played a decisive part in shaping the law of marriage and succeeded in establishing several basic principles still in force today (monogamy, marriage by consensus of the spouses, prohibition of marriage among relatives, indissolubility of marriage). In order to carry through these ideas the medieval Church claimed the exclusive right to legislate and administer justice in the core areas of marriage law. Even where the secondary effects of marriage were concerned church and state courts competed with each other.

6. Since the Reformation Germany is divided denominationally. The Reformers proclaimed a marriage theology which differed from the traditional Catholic view and marriage law from then on developed separately according to the denominations. This did not prevent the lasting influence of the church: in Protestant towns and states also theological convictions continued to form the basis of marriage law legislation (divorce only for reasons allowed in the bible, the requirement of parental consent for the marriage of children, etc.).

7. The growing importance of the state as opposed to the church and the ideas developing in the age of enlightenment led to an increasing profanation of family law from the 18th century onwards: Even in Catholic regions, the state now claimed the legal competence in the entire area of family law including marriage law. Marriage and family law were reformed according to the principles of secular legal policy. This was mirrored in the introduction of a secular marriage ceremony ('civil marriage') in the course of the 19th century.

8. The situation in the 19th century was characterized by extreme legal diversity as the individual German states all followed separate systems of law. Decisive steps on the way to German legal uniformity were the Law on Civil Status (Personenstandsgesetz) of 1875 and the Civil Code (Bürgerliches Gesetzbuch) of 18 August 1896. Since then, Germany has known a uniform family law which applies without reservation to persons of all religions. In principle, the law of the churches today is of no importance to the legal order of the state.

§3. SOURCES OF FAMILY AND SUCCESSION LAW

I. Constitution

9. Germany's constitution is laid down in the Basic Law (Grundgesetz, GG) of 23 May 1949. When it became the constitution for West Germany in 1949, the name was chosen to mark the temporary nature in a situation still awaiting German reunification. Since 1990 the Basic Law has served as the constitution for all of Germany. The constitutional guarantees and regulations as laid down in its 141 clauses are of central importance for legislation and jurisprudence in all areas of civil law, and thus also for Family Law.

10. German Family Law is shaped especially by the constitutional guarantee of Art. 6 GG, which places marriage and the family under the special protection of the state.[1] Likewise, the Basic Law safeguards the right to inherit; content and limits of this right are determined by statute law.[2] The law of persons as well as all other areas of law have to comply with certain fundamental values laid down in the constitution:

- The dignity of man shall be inviolable. To respect and to protect it shall be the duty of all state authority.[3]
- Everyone shall have the right to the free development of his personality in so far as he does not violate the rights of others or offends against the constitutional order or the moral code.[4]
- Everyone shall have the right to life and to the inviolability of his person. The liberty of the individual shall be inviolable.[5]
- All persons shall be equal before the law.[6]
- Men and women shall have equal rights.[7]
- No one may be prejudiced or favoured because of his sex, his parentage, his race, his language, his homeland and origin, his faith, or his religious or political opinions.[8]
- Freedom of faith, of conscience, and freedom of creed, religious or ideological, shall be inviolable.[9]

On this basis, the rulings of the Federal Constitutional Court (Bundesverfassungs-gericht, BVerfG) have substantially influenced the development of Family Law in Germany.

1. Art. 6 I GG, for details *cf. infra* No. 61
2. Art. 14 I 1 GG.
3. Art. 1 I GG.
4. Art. 2 I GG.
5. Art. 2 II GG.
6. Art. 3 I GG.
7. Art. 3 II 1 GG.
8. Art. 3 III GGG.
9. Art. 4 I GG

II. Legislation

11. German Family and Succession Law is mainly set down in the Civil Code (Bürgerliches Gesetzbuch, BGB) of 18 August 1896, in force since 1 Janaury 1900. The enactment of the Civil Code ended the extreme diversification of legal rules and systems which had lasted until the 19th century.

12. A new split in the legal system occurred after the Second World War with the division of Germany into the western Federal Republic of Germany and the eastern German Democratic Republic. Reflecting the Cold War-split between Eastern and Western political systems the two states developed very different political, economic and social institutions and the same was true for the legal systems: Whereas West-Germany retained the Civil Code and developed it further by reforming it, the GDR abolished the BGB and instead enacted new codes in the area of civil law.[1] Following the example of other socialist countries, East-German Family Law was completely reshaped according to socialist dogma and laid down in a new Family Law Code (Familiengesetzbuch, FGB).[2]

1. Zivilgesetzbuch (ZGB) der Deutschen Demokratischen Republik vom 19 June 1975 (Gbl. I No. 27 S. 465); Vertragsgesetz vom 25 March 1982 (Gbl. I No. 14 S. 293).
2. Familiengesetzbuch (FGB) der Deutschen Demokratischen Republik vom 20 December 1965 (Gbl. I 1966 No. 1 S. 1), reformiert durch Gesetz vom 20 July 1990 (Gbl. S.1038).

13. This division only ended with the German Reunification of 1990. On the basis of the Reunification Treaty of 31 August 1990, on 3 October 1990 the GDR acceded to the Federal Republic and adopted its laws. Both the Civil Code (BGB) and the Basic Law were thus (re-) introduced to the area of the former GDR and East-Berlin.

14. For law reform pertaining to Family and Inheritance Law we refer to the special chapters *infra*.[1]

1. Family Law: *see infra* No. 57 *sqq.*; Inheritance Law *see infra* No. 324 *sqq.*

III. Treaties

15. Germany has ratified a number of international and European treaties with relevance to the area of Family and Inheritance Law. Generally, an international treaty only becomes part of German domestic law upon its transformation into German Federal Law. The Basic Law rules that where a treaty relates to matters of federal legislation – as it is the case in the area of family and inheritance law – it shall require the consent or participation in the form of a federal law, of the bodies competent in the specific case for such federal legislation.[1]

1. Art. 59 II 1 Basic Law.

16. Of special importance to our area are the following international treaties that Germany has ratified:

– The Hague Convention relating to the Settlement of Guardianship of Minors (12 June 1902).
– The European Convention for the Protection of Human Rights and Fundamental Freedoms (4 November 1950).
– The Hague Convention on the Law Applicable to Maintenance Obligations towards Children (24 October 1956).

- The Hague Convention on the Recognition and Enforcement of Decisions relating to Maintenance Obligations towards Children (15 April 1958).
- The Hague Convention concerning the Powers of Authorities and the Law Applicable in respect of the Protection of Minors (5 October 1961).
- The Hague Convention on Jurisdiction, Applicable Law and Recognition of Decrees relating to Adoption (15 November 1965).
- The European Convention on the Adoption of Children (24 April 1967).
- The Hague Convention on the Recognition of Divorces and Legal Separation (1 June 1970).
- The Hague Convention on the Recognition and Enforcement of Decisions relating to Maintenance Obligations (2 October 1973).
- The European Convention on Recognition and Enforcement of Decisions concerning Custody of Children and on Restoration of Custody of Children (20 May 1980).
- The Hague Convention on the Civil Aspects of International Child Abduction (25 October 1980).
- The United Nations Convention on the Rights of the Child (20 November 1989).
- The Hague Convention on Protection of Children and Co-operation in Respect of Inter-Country Adoption (29 May 1993).
- The Hague Convention on the Conflicts of Laws relating to the Form of Testamentary Dispositions (5 October 1961).

IV. Case Law

17. Under German law previous decisions of higher courts are not, as a rule, binding on lower courts. Still, important and recent decisions of high-ranking courts such as the Federal Supreme Court (BGH) are regarded as persuasive and will in practice generally be followed, as otherwise the decision of the lower court is likely to be reversed on appeal. Even so, courts may be willing to depart from a previous line of authority, i.e. if this seems out of date and in the absence of a doctrine of *stare decisis* they are free to do so.

§4. THE COURTS ADMINISTERING FAMILY AND SUCCESSION LAW

18. With respect to the often sensitive nature of the issues in question and the important role that courts play in the area of Family Law, Germany – like many other countries – has entrusted a special division of the civil courts to deal with Family Law matters. In 1976[1] thus the 'Family Law Court' was introduced as a division of the County Court (Amtsgericht), the lowest court of record in Germany.[2] The Judge here is sitting alone.

1. First Marriage Law Act 1976 (1. EheRG).
2. §23b Judicature Act (Gerichtsverfassungsgesetz, GVG).

19. Appeals from there will go to the Higher Regional Courts (Oberlandes-gerichte). Here also special senates have been established which are responsible for Family Law matters (Familiensenate).[1] The next instance of appeal – on points of law only – is the Federal Court of Justice (Bundesgerichtshof, BGH), which has its seat in Karlsruhe (Baden-Württemberg).

    1. §119 II GVG.

20. The individual matters over which the Family Law Courts have jurisdiction are set out in a catalogue in the Judicature Act.[1] Its range has been substantially broadened by law reform in 1997/1998. Further jurisdiction exists in the area of non-contentious matters (Freiwillige Gerichtsbarkeit, FGG) as e.g. laid down in §1666 BGB.

    1. §23b I GVG.

21. Next to the family law courts stand the Guardianship Courts (Vormundschaftsgerichte), which are mainly concerned with the areas of guardian-ship, curatorship and care and control. As Guardianship Court acts a department of the competent County Court.

22. Inheritance Law is dealt with by the general civil law courts. Depending on the sum involved that means proceedings will start either at the County- or Regional Court (Landgericht, LG). On appeal the case will respectively go to the Regional or Higher Regional Court and only in the latter case further to the Federal Court of Justice.

23. The highest court in the country is the Federal Constitutional Court (Bundesverfassungsgericht, BVerfG), situated in Karlsruhe (Baden-Württemberg). It interprets the Basic Law in relation to individual rights, to disputes between the states and the federation and to legislation and may act e.g. on appeal by lower courts, government institutions and legislatures or private citizens. It has ruled extensively on questions of Family Law and initiated law reforms in many areas to ensure compatibility with the parameters of the Basic Law (e.g. on legislation per-taining to joint parental care of divorcees or on cohabitation).

Selected Bibliography

Family Law

Books:

Bäumel, D. et al., *Familienrechtsrformkommentar*, 1998.

Baumeister, W., et al., *Familiengerichtsbarkeit*, 1992.

Bergerfurth, B., *Der Ehescheidungsprozeß*, 11th ed., 1998.

Bergschneider, L., *Verträge in Familiensachen*, 1998.

Börger, U., *Eheliches Güterrecht*, 1989.

Bosch, F.W., *Gesammelte Abhandlungen zum Familien- und Erbrecht*, 1991.

Brambring, G., *Ehevertrag und Vermögenszuordnung unter Ehegatten*, 3rd ed., 1997.

Coester, M., *Das Kindeswohl als Rechtsbegriff*, 1982.

Gerhard, P., von Heintschel-Heinegg, B, and Klein, M. (eds.), *Handbuch des Fachanwalts Familienrecht*. 2nd ed., 1999.

Gernhuber, J. and Coester-Waltjen, D., *Lehrbuch des Familienrechts*, 4th ed., 1994.

Göppinger, H. and Wax, P., *Unterhaltsrecht*, 6th ed., 1994.

Göppinger, H. and Börger, U. (eds.), *Vereinbarungen anläßlich der Ehescheidung*, 7th ed., 1998.

Grziwotz, H., *Nichteheliche Lebensgemeinschaft*, 3rd ed., 1999.

Kalthoener, E., Büttner, H. and Niepmann, B., *Die Rechtsprechung zur Höhe des Unterhalts*, 7th ed., 2000.

Giesen, D., *Familienrecht*, 2nd ed., 1997.

Hausmann, R. and Hohloch, G. (eds.), *Das Recht der nichtehelichen Lebensgemeinschaft*, 1999.

Henrich, D., *Familienrecht*, 5th ed., 1995.

Henrich, D., *Internationales Scheidungsrecht*, 1998.

Hepting, R., *Ehevereinbarungen*, 1984.

Hinz, M., *Kindesschutz als Rechtsschutz und elterliches Sorgerecht*, 1976.

Hoppenz, R., *Familiensachen*, 6th ed., 1998.

Jayme, E., *Die Familie im Recht der unerlaubten Handlungen*, 1971.

Johannsen, K. and Henrich, D. (eds.), *Eherecht*, 3rd ed., 1998.

Langenfeld, G., *Der Ehevertrag*, 8th ed., 1998.

Langenfeld, G., *Handbuch der Eheverträge und Scheidungsvereinbarungen*, 4th ed., 2000.

Lieb, M., *Die Ehegattenmitarbeit im Spannungsfeld zwischen Rechtsgeschäft, Bereicherungsausgleich und gesetzlichem Güterstand*, 1970.

Selected Bibliography

Lipp, M., *Die ehelichen Pflichten und ihre Verletzung – ein Beitrag zur Fortbildung des persönlichen Eherechts*, 1988.
Lipp, M. and Wagenitz, Th., *Das neue Kindschaftsrecht*, 1999.
Lüderitz, A., *Familienrecht*, 27th ed., 1999.
Mikat, P., *Rechtsprobleme der Schlüsselgewalt*, 1981.
Müller-Freienfels, W., *Ehe und Recht*, 1962.
Pawlowski, H.-M., *Abschied von der 'Bürgerlichen Ehe'?*, Juristenzeitung 1998, 1032.
Pawlowski, H.-M., *Die 'Bürgerliche Ehe' als Organisation*, 1983.
Rahm, W. and Künkel, B. (eds.), *Handbuch des Familiengerichtsverfahrens*, 4th ed., 1997.
Schlüter, W., *BGB – Familienrecht*, 8th ed., 1998.
Scholz, H. and Stein, R., *Praxishandbuch Familienrecht*, 1998
Schwab, D., *Familienrecht*, 10th ed., 1999.
Schwab, D. (ed.), *Handbuch des Scheidungsrechts*, 4th ed., 2000.
Schwab, D. (ed.), *Das neue Familienrecht*, 1998.
Schwab, D. and Wagenitz, Th., *Familienrechtliche Gesetze*, 3rd ed., 1999.
Schwenzer, I., *Vom Status zur Realbeziehung*, 1987.
Simitis, S. and Zenz, G., *Seminar: Familie und Familienrecht*, 1975.
Simitis, S. et al., *Kindeswohl*, 1979.
Wendl, P. and Staudigl, S., *Das Unterhaltsrecht in der familienrichterlichen Praxis*, 5th ed., 2000.
Wagenitz, Th. and Bornhofen, H., *Handbuch des Eheschließungsrechts*, 1998.
Wagenitz, Th. and Bornhofen, H., *Familiennamensrechtsgesetz*, 1994.
Wever, R., *Vermögensauseinandersetzung der Ehegatten außerhalb des Güterrechts*, 2nd ed., 2000.
Zenz, G., *Kindesmißhandlung und Kindesrechte*, 1979.

Journals:

Zeitschrift für das gesamte Familienrecht (FamRZ)
Familie und Recht (FuR)
Familie Partnerschaft Recht (FuR)
Kindschaftsrechtliche Praxis (Kind-Prax)
Das Standesamt (StAZ)
Recht der Jugend und des Bildungswesens (RdJ)
Zentralblatt für Jugendrecht (ZfJ)
Der Amtsvormund (DAVorm)

Succession Law

a. Textbooks

Brox, *Erbrecht*, 18th ed. 2000 (Heymann).
Ebenroth, *Erbrecht*, 1992 (Beck).

Ebenroth/Auer, 'The Law of Succession', in: Ebke/Finkin, *Introduction to German Law*, 1996, 273 (Kluwer).

Frank, *Erbrecht*, 2000 (Beck).

Gursky, *Erbrecht*, 3rd ed. 1999 (Schaeffers Grundriss, C.F. Müller).

Harder, *Grundzüge des Erbrechts*, 4th ed. 1997 (Luchterhand).

Kipp/Coing, *Erbrecht*, 14th ed. 1990 (Mohr).

Lange/ Kuchinke, *Erbrecht*, 4th ed. 1995 (Beck).

Leipold, *Erbrecht*, 13th ed. 2000 (Mohr).

Michalski, *BGB-Erbrecht*, 1999 (C.F. Müller).

Schlüter, *Erbrecht*, 14th ed. 2000 (Beck).

b. Handbooks

Bengel/Reimann, *Handbuch der Testamentsvollstreckung*, 2nd ed. 1998.

Bock/Bünger/Fritz/U. Gottwald, *Praxishandbuch Erbrecht, Looseleaf* (Vol. 3), 2000.

Dittmann/Reimann/Bengel, *Testament und Erbvertrag*, 3rd ed. 2000.

Ebeling/Geck/Grune, *Handbuch der Erbengemeinschaft*, 6th ed. (Looseleaf).

Ferid/Firsching/Dörner/Hausmann, *Internationales Erbrecht*, Looseleaf (6 Vol.), 2000.

Firsching/Graf, *Nachlassrecht*, 8th ed. 2000.

Möhring/Beisswingert/Klingelhöffer, *Vermögensverwaltung in Vormundschafts- und Nachlasssachen*, 7th ed. 1992.

Nieder, *Handbuch der Testamentsgestaltung*, 2nd ed. 2000.

c. Commentaries

Detailed explanations to all rules of the law of succession are to be found in:

Erman, *BGB*, 10th ed. 2000.

Jauernig, *BGB*, 9th ed. 1999.

Münchener Kommentar zum BGB, Vol. 9, 3rd ed. 1997.

Palandt, *BGB*, 59th ed. 2000.

Soergel, *BGB*, Vol. 9, 12th ed. 1992.

Staudinger, *BGB*, 13th ed. 1994ff.

d. Case books

Heldrich, *Fälle und Lösungen: Erbrecht*, 3rd ed. 1989 (C.F. Müller).

Holzhauser, *Familien- und Erbrecht*, 2nd ed. 1988.

A. Roth, *Familien- und Erbrecht* (Jurathek Repetitorium), 2nd ed. 1999 (C.F. Müller).

Schlüter, *PdW BGB Erbrecht*, 8th ed. 1994 (Beck).

Simon/Werner, *21 Probleme aus dem Familien- und Erbrecht*, 2nd ed. 1991 (Metzner).

Werner, *Fälle zum Erbrecht*, 2nd ed. 1995 (Beck).

Selected Bibliography

e. General reading

W. Friedrich, *Testament und Erbrecht*, 18th ed. 1998 (dtv).
A. Frieser, *Was tun im Erbfall?*, 2nd ed. 1996 (dtv).
G. Mersson/G. Graz, *Beck-Ratgeber Vererben und erben*, 1997.
K. Winkler, *Erbrecht von A-Z*, 8th ed. 2000 (dtv).
W. Zimmermann, *Rechtsfragen bei einem Todesfall*, 2nd ed. 1995 (dtv).

f. Specialized law journals

FamRZ – Zeitschrift für das gesamte Familienrecht (mit Erbrecht), Gieseking (since 1953).
ZEV – Zeitschrift für Erbrecht und Vermögensnachfolge, Beck (since 1994).

Part I. Persons

Chapter 1. The Status of a Person

§1 Definition of a Person

24. German law distinguishes between 'natural' and 'legal' persons. Every human being is a natural person. Legal persons are certain associations of persons and other organizations, to which the law ascribes personal qualities in the legal sense.

25. Every human being enjoys legal capacity (*Rechtssubjekt*), i.e. may be the subject of rights and duties. Legal capacity also includes the ability to stand as a party in legal proceedings.[1] Legal capacity begins with the completion of birth,[2] i.e. with the complete separation of the child from the mother's body. In principle, all natural persons enjoy the same legal capacity: every human being may attain and exercise the same kinds of rights. This is true also in relation to gender: the Basic Law guarantees that men and women shall have equal rights in all areas of the law.[3]

   1. §50 I ZPO.
   2. §1 BGB.
   3. Art. 3 II, III GG.

26. The unborn child (*nasciturus*) does not enjoy legal capacity under German law. Still, the constitution protects the human dignity and an own right to life of the unborn child as well.[1] This protection of the *nasciturus* is mainly effected by provisions under criminal law.[2] Under civil law, on the other hand, the unborn child cannot be the subject of rights and the addressee of duties.

   1. BVerfGE 88, 203.
   2. *Cf.* §§218ff of the German Penal Code (Strafgesetzbuch, StGB).

27. Some provisions of the Civil Code, though, do protect the interests of the unborn child in the case that he is born alive later: §1923 II BGB rules that a person not yet living, but conceived at the time of the accrual of an inheritance is deemed to have been born before this accrual, i.e. may be heir. The provision will only apply, though, if the child is born alive. To protect the future rights of the unborn child a curator may be appointed to such extent as these require care.[1]

   1. §1912 BGB.

28. The legal capacity of a natural person ends with his death. Where the domicile of a person has been unknown for a longer time without any information on whether he is dead or alive, such a missing person may be **declared dead** under certain circumstances.[1] The official declaration of death leads to a rebuttable presumption that the missing person has actually died at the time stated in the order. Even though a person may not be the subject of rights and duties after his death, according to German jurisdiction personal rights (e.g. the right to privacy) continue even after death and may be asserted before a court by a trustee named by the deceased before his death or by his relatives.[2]

1. Law on Missing Persons of 15 January 1951 (Verschollenheitsgesetz).
2. *Cf.* BGHZ 50, 133 – Gustav Gründgens; BGH NJW 1990, 1986 – Emil Nolde.

29. German law knows the following legal persons:

1. The **Association with legal capacity** ('rechtsfähiger Verein'). An Association is an organization of persons the existence of which is not affected by a change in the membership. An Association whose object is not directed at the carrying out of an economic enterprise acquires legal personality by registration in the Register of Associations of the competent District Court.[1]
2. The **Foundation with legal capacity** ('rechtsfähige Stiftung'). Under German law, this represents an organization in which the property assigned to the foundation is directed at a certain purpose, e.g. in the social sphere. The Foundation gains legal capacity by authorization of the state.[2]
3. The **Public Limited Company** ('Aktiengesellschaft', AG).[3]
4. The **Limited Liability Company** ('Gesellschaft mit beschränkter Haftung', GmbH).[4]
5. The **Registered Trade and Industrial Co-operatives** ('eingetragene Erwerbs- und Wirtschaftsgenossenschaft').[5]

1. §21 BGB.
2. §80 BGB.
3. Company law (Aktiengesetz, AktG) of 6 September 1965.
4. Limited Liability Company Act (GmbH-Gesetz) of 20 April 1892.
5. Co-operative Societies Act (Genossenschaftsgesetz) of 1 May 1889.

30. Furthermore, German law knows associations of persons which are of only **partial** legal capacity, e.g. the **General Partnership** ('Offene Handelsgesellschaft', OHG). Under its firm name, the General Partnership may acquire rights, enter into obligations, acquire property and property rights, take legal action and be sued. The Partners are liable not only with the company's property, but also personally.[1] Partial legal capacity is also a trademark of the **Limited Partnership** ('Kommanditgesellschaft', KG).[2] Whether other personal associations as the **Partnership under civil law** ('Gesellschaft bürgerlichen Rechts')[3] enjoy (partial) legal capacity is the subject of much debate among German courts and in legal writing.

1. §128 Commercial Code (Handelsgesetzbuch, HGB).
2. §161 *sq.* Commercial Code (HGB).
3. §705 *sq.* BGB.

§2. Capacity

I. General

31. Under German law, the ability to effect legal consequences by declarations (e.g. to enter into a contract) is termed 'capacity to enter into legal transactions' ('Geschäftsfähigkeit'). In principle, every human being is legally competent. Exceptions are made where (a) a person has not yet reached eighteen years of age and (b) where a person suffers from a pathological mental disturbance which prevents the free exercise of his will unless this condition is temporary in nature.[1]

   1. §104 BGB.

II. Minors

32. Minors, i.e. persons who have not yet reached the age of eighteen, are either incompetent or partially competent to enter into legal transactions.

Children are **incompetent to enter into legal transactions** if they have not yet completed their seventh year of age.[1] Any declaration made by a legally incompetent person is void.[2] A declaration made to a person who is legally incompetent is not effective until it reaches his legal representative.[3]

Minors are **limited in capacity to enter into legal transactions** if they have completed their seventh year of age but not yet their eighteenth.[4] As a rule, a person who is of limited legal capacity may make declarations of intent. Their validity will depend on the assent (prior consent ('Einwilligung') or later approval ('Genehmigung')) of his legal representative.[5]

   1. §104 No. 1 BGB.
   2. §105 BGB.
   3. §131 I BGB.
   4. If they are not legally incompetent under §104 No. 1 BGB.
   5. §§107–113 BGB.

33. Minors in principle have a '**legal representative**'. As a rule, this will be the parents, to the extent that they have parental care, otherwise a curator or guardian will act as legal representative.[1]

   1. §1629 BGB.

III. Majors

34. A person is legally incompetent if he suffers from a pathological mental disturbance preventing the free exercise of his will, unless this condition is temporary in nature.[1] Whether such a condition existed has to be affirmed in each particular case, e.g. when trying to determine the validity of a contract. Legal incompetence may also exist only in relation to certain transactions (partial incompetence). Incapacity to enter into legal transactions has to be proven by the person claiming it. Since 1992 it is no longer possible to place someone under guardianship, i.e. to declare him as generally legally incompetent by way of court order.

    1.   §104 No. 2 BGB.

35. Conditions which are only temporary in nature will not lead to legal incapacity, the same is true for the state of unconsciousness, although a declaration of intent made in such a condition is void.[1]

    1.   §105 II BGB.

36. If it is necessary to appoint a protector for a person (*see infra* No. 242 *sqq.*), the protector represents the person under his care in judicial and extrajudicial matters.[1] This does not limit the general legal capacity of the person under care. In order to avert substantial jeopardy to the person under care the court may order that prior consent of the protector shall be necessary ('reservation of consent').[2] The consequence is that within a certain scope of action the person under care may only act with the consent of the protector.[3]

    1.   §1902 BGB.
    2.   §1903 BGB.
    3.   §1903 1 2; §§108ff., 131 II BGB.

IV. Consent to Undergo Medical Treatment

37. Different rules apply where a person's consent to undergo medical treatment is concerned. German courts assume that here legal capacity is not the decisive factor. Instead, a person may validly consent to a medical treatment if he is able to understand the importance and consequences of the treatment ('natural understanding'). Depending on the medical measure in question this might be assumed for minors starting from the age of fourteen to sixteen years. Likewise, a person under care may possibly have the necessary understanding to consent to medical treatment himself. The question is not regulated by statute. It is therefore a matter of debate whether e.g. a woman who has not yet come of age may consent to the termination of her pregnancy without the assent of her parents.

V. Responsibility for Delict under Civil Law

38. According to the German law of delict, a person who has not yet completed his seventh year of age is not responsible for any damage which he causes to another.[1] Where a person has completed the seventh year of age but not yet the eighteenth, he will only be responsible for a damage which he causes to another if he, at the time of committing the damaging act, did have the understanding necessary for realizing his responsibility.[2]

    1.   §828 I BGB.
    2.   §828 II BGB.

39. A person who was unconscious or who suffered from a mental disturbance which prevented the free exercise of his will when acting is not responsible for the damage caused to another. This is different if he has brought himself into such a temporary condition by alcoholic drinks or similar means.[1] A person who is thus not responsible for the damage caused under the rules named *supra* may nevertheless have to compensate for the damages if equity requires this.[2]

   1. §827 BGB.
   2. §829 BGB.

VI. Criminal Responsibility

40. A child does not attain criminal responsibility before he has completed the age of fourteen.[1] A juvenile between the age of fourteen and eighteen is criminally responsible if at the time of committing the delinquency he was of sufficient mental and moral maturity to understand the wrong of the deed and to act accordingly.[2] Juveniles and majors between the age of eighteen and twenty-one will be tried before a special court (Juvenile Court) and under special procedural rules.

   1. §1 II Juvenile Courts Act (Jugendgerichtsgesetz, JGG) of 11 December 1974.
   2. §3 JGG.

§3. ABSENTEES

41. An absent person of full age whose whereabouts are unknown receives for his property affairs, as far as those need care, a curator ('Abwesenheitspfleger').[1] The same applies to an absent person whose whereabouts are known but who is prevented from returning and taking care of his property affairs.[2] A person who is missing may under certain circumstances be declared legally dead.

   1. §1911 I BGB.
   2. §1911 II BGB.

Chapter 2. Registration of Civil Status

§1. THE REGISTRAR

42. The Registrar's office records the civil status and is responsible for the Register of Civil Status.[1] These tasks are conferred to the Local Authorities.[2] There is a large number of Registrar's Office Districts ('Standesamtsbezirke') across the country which all have to be equipped with a sufficient number of Registrars. Every Municipality belongs to a certain Registrar's Office District.

> 1. §1 I Law on Civil Status (Personenstandsgesetz, PStG) of 8 August 1957.
> 2. §51 PStG.

§2. REGISTERS AND CERTIFICATES

43. The Registrar is responsible for keeping the following registers:

– The Marriage Register, in which all wedding ceremonies are recorded.
– The Family Register, the recordings of which concern the whole family (spouses, parents of the spouses, common or adopted children, death of a spouse, divorce, changes of name, etc.).
– The Birth Register, in which the name and sex of a child and the day, hour and place of his birth are recorded.
– The Death Register, which records all cases of deaths.

On the basis of the civil status registers the Registrar issues specific documents, e.g. Birth, Marriage, or Death Certificates.

The Civil Status Registers provide proof of wedding ceremonies, births and deaths and further details recorded in the context, but not about questions of nationality.[1] Proof established by the Civil Status Registers may be rebutted.

> 1. §60 I PStG.

Chapter 3. Personality Rights

44. See supra No. 24 *sqq.*

Chapter 4. Names

§1. COMPOSITION OF A NAME (FIRST NAME, SURNAME, INDIVIDUAL NAME, TITLE OF
NOBILITY)

45. German law protects the name of a person as a part of his identity. Whoever
legitimately bears a name may take action against others using it or against
someone who disputes his right to bear that name. If further infringements are to be
feared he may seek an injunction.[1] Whoever is injured in his right of name may
claim compensation for the arising damage from the responsible person.[2]

1. §12 RGB.
2. §823 BGB.

46. 'Names' in the sense of the above are mainly the first name and the surname.
It should be noted that in Germany marks of nobility (titles) count as part of the
surname (e.g. Prinz von Adlersberg).[1] Pseudonyms, *noms de plume* or stage names
are equally protected as well as coats of arms or seals, which stand for a person's
identity. Protected are further the name of legal entities or other associations of
persons, the name of a merchant ('firm name'), as well as abbreviations which have
come to characterize a certain business (e.g. BMW).

1. This finds its reason in the Weimar Constitution of 11 August 1919.

§2. SURNAME

I. Acquisition of the Surname

47. The surname is either the 'birth-name' or the name acquired upon marriage.
A child acquires his surname upon his birth either by act of law or because his parents
or other persons who have parental care determine it. Because the right to name a
child depends on the question of parental care the rather complicated rules governing the child's name are dealt with in Part II (Family Law), *cf. infra* No. 158*sq.* The
surname may change during the lifetime, e.g. because of marriage (*see infra*
No. 101 *sqq.*), divorce (*see infra* No. 104 *sqq.*) or adoption (*see infra* No. 169).

II. Change of the Surname

48. In addition to the rules under civil law the possibility exists to change the
surname by way of an official procedure. A surname may only be changed if
serious reasons require this,[1] e.g. if the name causes ridicule.

1. §3 Act on the change of names (Namensänderungsgesetz) of 5 January 1938.

§3. FIRST NAME

49. A child's first name is chosen either by his parents or by other persons who have parental care (*see infra* No. 172 *sqq.*). A child can carry more than one first name. The Registrar may refuse to record a first name which is not common; his decision is appealable before the courts.[1] Also, the first name can be changed by official procedure, the same conditions apply as in the case of a change of surname.[2]

1. §45 PStG.
2. §11 Namensänderungsgesetz.

Chapter 5. Nationality

50. The German nationality is acquired either by birth or by naturalization. A child will acquire the German nationality by birth if one of his parents is a German national. Where only the father is a German national it may be necessary to prove or to acknowledge his paternity.[1]

If both parents are foreign nationals and the child is born in Germany he is granted German nationality if one his parents has lived in Germany for eight years and is in possession of a valid residence permit ('Aufenthaltsberechtigung') or for three years has had a right to reside ('Aufenthaltserlaubnis').[2]

    1.   §4 I Citizenship Act (Staatsangehörigkeitsgesetz) of 22 July 1913.
    2.   §4 III Staatsangehörigkeitsgesetz.

51. Furthermore, a child acquires German nationality if he is formally and law-fully adopted by a German national according to German law.[1] The child must be under the age of eighteen at the time of lodging the application for an adoption order.

The possibility to acquire German nationality by naturalization[2] has been facilitated by recent reform.[3] A special easing of terms applies for spouses of German nationals.[4]

    1.   §6 Staatsangehörigkeitsgesetz.
    2.   *Cf.* §§8–15 Staatsangehörigkeitsgesetz.
    3.   *Cf.* the Gesetz zur Reform des Staatsangehörigkeitsrechts of 15 July 1999, BGBl. I, p. 1618.
    4.   *Cf.* §9 Staatsangehörigkeitsgesetz.

Chapter 6. Domicile and Residence

52. German law knows both permanent residence ('Wohnsitz') and domicile ('ständiger Aufenthalt'). A person who abides regularly in a place establishes his **residence** there.[1] A person's permanent residence is the place (the municipality) where he is established permanently. A subjective element is also necessary: he must be willing to establish the centre of his life there (intent to residence). A cursory stay will not result in a permanent residence. The residence ends if the abode is abandoned with the intention of discontinuing it.[2] Residence may exist simultaneously in several places.[3]

1. §7 I BGB.
2. §7 III BGB.
3. §7 II BGB.

53. A person who is legally incompetent or who is limited in capacity to enter into legal transactions may neither establish nor abandon a residence without the consent of his legal representative.[1] An exception is made for a minor who is married; he may independently establish or abandon a residence.[2] By act of law, a minor child shares the residence of his parents if they have parental care. If neither of his parents has the right to parental care, the child will share the residence of whoever does have that right.[3]

1. §8 I BGB.
2. §8 II BGB.
3. §11 BGB.

54. The term '**domicile**' has a similar meaning to that of 'residence'. It means the factual centre of life of a person[1] and it is established by a longer actual stay at that place.[2] Different from residence, here it is not necessary that a person acts with the intention to establish his centre of life somewhere. Unlike in the case of residence, the domicile of a child thus is not automatically identical with that of his parents.[3]

1. BGH FamRZ 1981, 135, 136.
2. BGH NJW 1983, 2771.
3. BGH FamRZ 1981, 135, 136.

55. Whether a certain question is decided according to the domicile or residence of a person depends on the relevant legal provision. Residence is of special importance e.g. in the area of private international law.[1]

1. *Cf.* §14 I No. 2, §15 II No. 2 EGBGB.

Chapter 7. Mentally Handicapped Persons

*56. See supr*a No. 34 *sqq.* and infra No. 222 *sqq.*

Part II. Family Law

Introductory Remarks

§1. THE COURSE OF LEGISLATION IN THE AREA OF FAMILY LAW

57. German family law has undergone manifold changes since it was codified in the *Civil Code* of 18 August 1896.[1] The main shifts were brought about by the following legislation:

> 1. Bürgerliches Gesetzbuch (BGB), in force since 1 January 1900.

58. – The *Marriage Act*,[1] issued under the Hitler Regime, changed the entire system of rules relating to the marriage ceremony and to divorce. In parts, the Act was influenced by national-socialist ideology.

  – The *Control Council Act* No. 16.[2] The Act issued by the Allied Control Council re-implemented the Marriage Act 1938 after it had been cleared of national-socialist influences.

  – The *Sex Discrimination Act*[3] aimed at restructuring family law according to the principle of gender equality but still in parts retained a traditional understanding of roles within marriages (e.g. modelling legislation on the assumption that the female role within marriage would be that of the housewife).

  – The *Family Code*,[4] enacted by the German Democratic Republic, separated family law from the general civil law in a way similar to other Eastern Block countries and reshaped it to conform with socialist dogma.

  – The *First Reform Act on Marriage and the Family*[5] established the Family Law Courts (Familiengerichte) as a special branch of the Lower Regional Courts (Landgerichte).

  – The *Parental Care Reform Act*[6] put the legal relationship between parents and children on a new basis, strengthening children's rights. The principle distinction between children born in and out of wedlock was retained.

  – The *Treaty on German Reunification*[7] introduced West-German family law to the territory of the ex-GDR.

  – The *Care and Control Act*[8] abolished guardianship over persons of age. Instead, it introduced Care and Control as a new legal framework to provide assistance to physically or mentally ailing persons ('Betreuung').

- The *Child Law Reform Act*[9] aimed at doing away with differing legal treatment of children born in and out of wedlock. Major adjustments were also made to parental care, especially relating to care after divorce or separation.
- The *Child Support Act*[10] reformed especially the procedures under which a child may claim financial support from his parents.
- The *Formation of Marriage Act*[11] comprised a complete redrafting of the law relating to the formation of marriage. Simultaneously, the Marriage Act 1938 was repealed. Since then, the substantive law rules governing Family Law are once again all to be found within the BGB (4th book: Family Law).

1. Ehegesetz (EheG), of 7 July 1938.
2. Kontrollratsgesetz, of 20 February 1946.
3. Gleichberechtigungsgesetz (GleichberG), of 18 June 1957.
4. Familiengesetzbuch (FGB), of 20 December 1965.
5. Erstes Gesetz zur Reform des Ehe- und Familienrechts (1. EheRG), of 14 June 1976.
6. Gesetz zur Neuregelung des Rechts der elterlichen Sorge (SorgeRG), of 18 July 1979.
7. Einigungsvertrag zwischen der Bundesrepublik Deutschland und der Deutschen Demokratischen Republik (Einig V), in force since 3 October 1990.
8. Betreuungsgesetz (BtG), of 12 December 1990.
9. Kindschaftsrechtsreformgesetz (KindRG), of 16 February 1997.
10. Kindesunterhaltsgesetz (KindUG), of 4 June 1998.
11. Eheschließungsrechtsgesetz (EheschlRG), of 4 May 1998.

§2. Family Law and the German Constitution (Basic Law)

59. The German Basic Law[1] provides a framework against which all rules relating to Family Law in Germany are to be measured. The most important provisions are found within Art. 6 and 3 of the Basic Law.

- Marriage and the family shall enjoy the special protection of the state.[2]
- Men and women enjoy equal rights;[3] nobody therefore may be discriminated against – or favoured – on the grounds of gender.[4] As interpreted by the Federal Constitutional Court (BVerfG), this principle of equal rights is applicable within marriage and the family[5] and is crucial in defining the legal structure of these institutions: It means that for legal purposes husband and wife are regarded as equals in marriage. This pertains to every aspect of married life, including the upbringing of children, the choosing of the married name or the distribution of work within the marriage, where e.g. gainful employment and the care for the family will be deemed as equal shares by the Courts.

It also means that the opinion of neither of the spouses will structurally take precedence, but that they both enjoy the same rights. In this light any legislation which in case of dispute confers a decisive vote generally e.g. to the husband (as was the case where the married couple could not agree on a family name) will be deemed to violate Art. 3 II, 6 I GG. The principle of equality applies within the family also, e.g. to the relation between sons and daughters.

1.   Grundgesetz (GG), of 23 May 1949; *cf. infra* No. 9*sq.*
2.   Art. 6 I GG.
3.   Art. 3 II GG.
4.   Art. 3 III GG.
5.   BVerfGE 3, 225.

60. – Care for and upbringing of children are the parents' natural right and a
        duty primarily incumbent on them.[1] It is the community's responsibility
        to ensure that they perform this duty.[2] Parental rights and duties are
        further specified in Art. 6 III GG: Thereafter, children may not be sepa-
        rated from their families against the will of their parents or guardians
        save in accordance with a law in cases where they fail in their duty or
        there is danger of the children being seriously neglected for other reasons.
    – Every mother is entitled to the protection and care of the community.[3]
    – Lastly, Art. 6 GG also determines the state's duty to ensure that children
       born out of wedlock shall be provided by law with the same opportunities
       for their physical and mental development and regarding their place in
       society as they are enjoyed by those born in marriage.[4]

1.   Art 6 II GG.
2.   Art. 6 II 2 GG.
3.   Art. 6 IV GG.
4.   Art. 6 V GG.

61. The Federal Constitutional Court has further clarified the threefold function
of these constitutional guarantees:

– Firstly, Art. 6 GG grants *individual rights* to married persons, parents, mothers
   and illegitimate children in the mode of classic civil liberties' protection, thus
   shielding the private sphere from undue interference by the state.
– Secondly, Art. 6 GG contains a guarantee of marriage and family *as institutions*
   ('Institutsgarantie'). In this capacity, according to the BVerfG, it safeguards only
   the essential features of marriage and the family, and sets out the standard with
   which the actual family law has to comply (e.g. principle of monogamy,
   freedom of marriage).
– But according to the BVerfG, the function fulfilled by Art. 6 GG goes even
   beyond this. Art. 6 GG also constitutes a fundamental norm, i.e. an imperative
   value to be observed in the entire area of private and public law as regards marriage and the family. The implications are twofold: on the one hand, it means
   that the state is prohibited from harming or impairing the institutions of marriage and family. On the other hand, the state is under a positive obligation to
   support both by appropriate means and to actively protect it from impairment by
   other forces. The BVerfG emphasizes, though, that this duty to support and
   protect does not extent to any specific claims made by individuals, e.g. to make
   good all financial burdens carried by the family.

62. Changing patterns of life have opened traditional definitions of terms like
'marriage' or 'family' to discussion. According to the BVerfG, the term marriage
still retains its original meaning as envisaged in 1949, referring exclusively to the

union between one man and one women, in principle intended for life.[1] 'Family' refers to the community between parents (or one parent) and children, embracing both illegitimate, adopted and step-children. Whether this community also includes the relationship between grandparents and grandchildren is still subject to dispute.

1.   BVerfGE 53, 224.

Chapter 1. Marriage

§1. The Engagement

I. Promise of Marriage

63. Under German law, the term 'engagement' holds a twofold meaning describing both the promise of marriage between a man and a woman and the legal relation established thereby. The engagement is contracted by a mutual promise carried by the earnest will to be bound for a future marriage. This promise can be given expressly or by conduct implying such an intent. Historically, German law knew complex actions for breach of promise of marriage. Today only limited rights are still ascribed to the engagement.

64. The exact legal nature of the promise of marriage has long been a subject of discussion in Germany. In any case, the code spells out that from an engagement no action follows for the envisaged marriage ceremony to be performed.[1] Such a judgement would also not be enforceable.[2] Any promised contractual penalties are void.[3]

1. §1297 BGB.
2. *See* §§888 III, 894 II ZPO.
3. §1297 II BGB.

II. Break-off of the Engagement

65. Where the engagement is broken off, gifts exchanged between the betrothed can be reclaimed according to the rules of unjust enrichment, §§1301, 812 *sqq.* BGB.

Should a fiancé(e) provoke the break-off of the engagement without good cause he/she is liable for damages, §§1298, 1299 BGB. A lack of good cause will be acknowledged by the Courts where the responsibility for the failed engagement lies solely in the sphere of this party, e.g. in the case of infidelity, serious misdemeanour, etc.

Under 1298 I 1 BGB the other fiancé(e), his/her parents or any other third party may claim refund for expenses made on the condition of the marriage taking place, e.g. for the planned marriage reception, the future common household, etc. The fiancé(e) may also recover damages for any further financial or professional arrangements made for the benefit of the forthcoming marriage under §1298 I 2 BGB, e.g. where notice has been given to an employer, assets were sold, etc. Only such expenses or other damages are recoverable, though, which were appropriate under the circumstances, §1298 II BGB. The party calling off the envisaged marriage thus will not be liable for ill-considered or disproportionate dispositions made by the other.[1]

1. *Cf.* BGH FamRZ 1961, 424.

66. Since the *Formation of Marriage Act 1998*[1] no more damages can be claimed by the fiancé as compensation for non-pecuniary damage resulting from the break-off of the engagement.

1. 'Eheschließungsrechtsgesetz' (EheschlRG).

67. Apart from the claims spelled out in 1298 *sqq.* BGB, German law generally recognizes the engagement as a special bond between the betrothed with resulting legal implications in other areas of law: e.g. fiancés may already conclude marriage agreements. Where contracts of inheritance are concerned, fiancés are viewed alike to spouses. Both civil and criminal procedure know special rights and rules for the engaged.[1]

1. *See* §383 1 No. 1 ZPO; §§52 I No. 1 StPO, 11 I No. 1a StGB.

§2. The Capacity to Marry

I. Competence to Enter into Legal Transactions (Geschäftsfähigkeit)

68. Under the doctrine of freedom of marriage,[1] restrictions relating to the capacity to marry have to be based on compelling reasons. As far as declarations of marriage are concerned, the general rules on competence to enter into legal transactions (§§104 *sqq.* BGB) have therefore been modified in the following way:

1. Art. 6 I GG.

69. – A person who is incompetent to enter into legal transactions (§104 BGB) may not enter into marriage, §1304 BGB. The wording of §1304 BGB is misleading in that a marriage concluded contrary to the provision will not be non-existent, but voidable, i.e. valid unless annulled with *ex nunc* effect, §1314 I BGB.

It should also be noted that incompetence to enter into legal transactions in the sense of §104 BGB may be only partial. It may thus be well possible that a person legally incompetent in other respects may still validly conclude a marriage. Proceedings for an annulment can be initiated by either of the spouses or the competent administrative authority, §1316 BGB. The legal representative will act for the incompetent spouse. An annulment is excluded, if the incompetence has ended and the formerly affected spouse has made it known that he wants to maintain the marriage, §1315 I 1 No. 2 BGB.

70. – The same rules apply to a person who is unconscious or temporarily in a state of mental disturbance when making the declaration, §1314 II No. 1 BGB.

II. Majority

71. As a rule, marriage shall not be entered into before the parties' attainment of majority. The Guardianship Court may give dispensation from this provision on specific application, if the applicant has completed the sixteenth year of age, and the applicant's intended spouse is of full age, §1303 I, II BGB. The legal representative of a minor or of a person who is limited in competency to enter into legal transactions for other reasons may successfully protest against such dispensation. Only if this protest is lodged without reasonable grounds, the Guardianship Court may issue a substitute order upon the petition of the engaged person who needs the consent.

72. The Registrar shall refuse his participation in a marriage ceremony sought for in violation of §1303 BGB. Where the marriage is nevertheless concluded, it is – appearances of §1303 BGB ('shall') to the contrary – voidable, §1314 I. Where a subsequent annulment is not possible because the legal representative's consent is withheld without reasonable grounds, the Guardianship Court may issue a substitute order as described *supra*.[1] Annulment is further excluded if the spouse, after he became legally competent, has made it known that he wants to maintain the marriage, §1315 I 1 No. 1 BGB.

1. *See* No. 71.

III. Failure of Intention

73. The declarations of marriage made by the nuptials may suffer from manifold failures of intention which may lead to the annulment of the marriage. Under the new law[1] the failures that constitute a ground for annulment have been substantially curtailed. They are to be found exclusively in §1314 II BGB, the general rules of §§116 *sqq.* BGB are not applicable to the declaration of marriage.

1. In force since 1 July 1998.

74. An annulment is only possible where there has been fraud, intimidation or mistake when making the declaration. Mistake will only constitute a ground for annulment if the spouse at the time of the marriage ceremony did not know that it was a matter of marriage at all, §1314 II No. 2 BGB. This may lead to surprising results: As long as the mistaken spouse knows he is partaking in a (any) marriage ceremony it is irrelevant to the validity of the marriage if he did not intend to give any marriage declaration or if he was mistaken as to the identity of the other spouse. Also, since 1 July 1998 a mistake as to the personal character of the other spouse does not constitute a ground of annulment any more.

IV. Fraud and Threats

75. Fraud will render the marriage voidable if a spouse was induced to enter into the marriage by fraud concerning conditions such as would have kept him from entering into the marriage had he known the real state of affairs and had correctly appraised the nature of the marriage. Fraud in this context is to be interpreted on the lines developed for §123 BGB, but the Code expressly exempts deceit concerning financial circumstances, §1314 II No. 3 Hs. 2 BGB. Also, where fraud was perpetrated by a third person it will only provide a ground for annulment under §1314 BGB if the other spouse had positive knowledge thereof, §1314 II No. 3 Hs.2 BGB.

It is important to note that according to long-standing interpretation by the Courts, concealment of relevant facts may be seen as fraud if there had been a duty to disclose.[1] Since mistake about the character of the other spouse does no longer form a separate ground of annulment it is to be expected that this interpretation by the Courts will gain new importance. It will thus be necessary to closely scrutinize in which cases a duty to disclose certain facts can legitimately be assumed.

1.   BGH, FamRZ 1958, 314.

76. Lastly, a spouse may petition for an annulment where he has been induced to enter into the marriage illegally by threats, §1314 II No. 4 BGB.

77. A petition for annulment may only be filed by the wronged spouse. The action must be brought within one year, taken from the point in time at which the relevant facts became known to the spouse, §1317 I BGB. In any case, an annulment is excluded if the spouse after the termination of the threat, the discovery of the fraud or the mistake has made it known that he wants to maintain the marriage, §1315 I BGB.

V. Fictitious Marriages

78. The *Formation of Marriage Act 1998*[1] introduced for the first time explicit rules on how to deal with fictitious marriages, i.e. with marriages contracted with the sole purpose to achieve secondary benefits (financial, residential, etc.).[2] According to §1314 II No. 5 BGB a marriage is voidable where the partners agreed never to live in conjugal community with each other. The Registrar is to refuse his participation where such an intent is obvious to him. If necessary, he is entitled to interview the partners accordingly and to ask for further evidence to be produced, §5 IV PStG. Should he be in doubt whether or not to participate in the marriage ceremony, he may apply to the court[3] for a decision,[4] §45 II PStG.

1.   Eheschließungsrechtsgesetz (EheschlRG).
2.   E.g. under §§17 *sqq.* AuslG.
3.   Local Court (Amtsgericht).
4.   §45 Law on Civil Status (Personenstandsgesetz, PStG).

79. A marriage voidable on the grounds of §1314 II No. 5 BGB can be annulled by Court order. The order will be effective *ex nunc* only. Applications for such an order of annulment may be made by the spouses or the relevant administrative authority, §1316 I No. 1 BGB. No order can be made though where the spouses – even if contrary to their prior intention – have actually lived together in conjugal community, §1315 I 1 No. 5 BGB, even if only for a short time.

VI. Impediments to Marriage

80. In the light of Art. 6 GG and the freedom of marriage, impediments to marriage imposed by the law have to have special justification. Accordingly, today only the last traces of an once extensive system of marriage impediments remain. The code distinguishes between such impediments as will lead to the marriage's voidability (but *ex nunc* effect only) and impediments that will not have any effect on the validity of the marriage.

1. §1306 BGB spells out that no marriage may be concluded where one of the partners is still married to a third party, even if this other marriage is voidable. This is only different where one of the partners is still validly married only because his divorce – although already pronounced – has not yet become unappealable.

   Other than in this particular case, any second marriage concluded contrary to §1306 BGB will be voidable, except where a spouse has wrongly been declared to be dead. Here, the new marriage may only be annulled if both new partners had known him to be still alive, §1319 BGB.
2. Affinity does no longer form an impediment to marriage. Since the *Formation of Marriage Act 1998* even the marriage between step-parent and step-child will thus be valid, §1590 I BGB.
3. Consanguinity constitutes an impediment in so far as it prevents the marriage between persons related in the direct line and between siblings, §1589 S.1 BGB. Thus today e.g. uncle and niece or two first cousins are free to marry. Violation of §1307 BGB will result in the marriage being voidable, i.e. valid unless annulled.
4. Where kinship had been established by adoption, the same rules apply as long as the adoption order is not revoked, §1308 BGB, with the exception that – even though the Registrar is to refuse the solemnization of such a marriage – a marriage nevertheless concluded in violation of §1308 BGB will be deemed valid.

VII. Annulment

81. Annulment of the marriage will be by Court order, §1313 I BGB and will be effective for the future only ('*ex nunc*'). Jurisdiction lies with the Family Law Court, the procedure is initiated on application of the relevant party or local authority, §1316 BGB. An annulment will only be granted on the grounds described *supra*, §§1313 S.3, 1314 I, II BGB. The annulment becomes effective when the Court order has become unappealable.

82. Similar to a divorce, the annulment of a marriage may lead to respective claims for maintenance, equalization of accrued gains and pension splitting, §1318 BGB. These claims follow special rules:

– Maintenance may be claimed by the injured party in a number of cases spelled out in the Code, e.g. in the instance of fraud or intimidation, §1318 II No. 1 BGB, or where there existed a ground for annulment according to §§1306, 1307 or 1311 BGB and both partners knew this. Even in the absence of such knowledge maintenance claims may be founded where common children are looked after, §1318 II 2 BGB.
– Equalization of accrued gains and pension splitting may not be claimed where such claims would seem grossly inequitable.
– Allocation of house-hold effects will be made according to the 'Hausrats-verordnung',[1] *cf.* §1318 IV BGB.
– As far as any children of the marriage are concerned, parental care, contact, etc. will follow the rules for separation and divorce. As in the case of divorce or separation, no automatic change in parental care is effected just by the annulment of the marriage.
– In Inheritance Law, the decree of nullity is allowed a certain retrospective effect. Under §§1318 V, 1931 BGB a spouse may be excluded from the right to intestate succession if the marriage was annulled on grounds of violation of §§1304, 1306, 1307, 1311 or §1314 II No. 2 BGB as described *supra* and if he was aware of the marriage's voidability.

    1.   *See infra* No. 129 *sqq.*

§3. FORMALITIES OF MARRIAGE

I. General

83. The freedom of marriage is a right guaranteed by the German constitution.[1] Nevertheless, the constitution entitles the legislator to lay down certain justifiable rules and formal requirements for the solemnization. Since the *Formation of Marriage Act 1998*[2] these rules are once again to be found in the BGB, the previously existing *Marriage Act*[3] having been abolished.

    1.   Art. 6 GG.
    2.   Eheschließungsrechtsgesetz (EheschlRG).
    3.   Ehegesetz (EheG), first introduced in 1938.

84. The celebration of marriage in Germany is a civil ceremony conducted before the Registrar. No other marriage ceremony (e.g. religious) will have legal effect. The Code lays down further requirements relating e.g. to capacity or formalities of the marriage. Where these requirements are not adhered to, the marriage will either be non-existent ('Nichtehe'), meaning that no valid marriage ever existed and no annulment proceedings need to be instituted, or *voidable* ('aufheb-bare Ehe'), meaning that the marriage is valid unless dissolved. It is important to note, though, that such dissolution will have 'ex nunc'-effect only, as German law as it stands today does not know retroactive dissolution anymore. The term 'voidable' therefore is used here to indicate a marriage which is valid, but may be dissolved with effect to the future.

II. The Marriage Ceremony

85. The celebration of marriage is preceded by a preparatory procedure before the locally competent Registrar. The parties must give notice to him of their intent to marry. Such notice must be accompanied by official documents proving the parties' descent.[1] The Registrar will inquire into any lawful impediments to the proposed marriage and may ask for further relevant proof, e.g. for a decree of divorce or a certificate of no impediment in the case of foreign law marriages. Where the Registrar is not satisfied that the parties are free to marry, he must refuse participation in the marriage ceremony. His decision is appealable.[2] All the above named formal requirements are directory provisions only, the violation of which will not hinder the contraction of a valid marriage.

   1. §§4, 5 PStG.
   2. §54 PStG.

86. The marriage is concluded by the declarations of the engaged persons before the Registrar that they want to contract marriage with each other, §1310 I 1, 1311 BGB. A marriage concluded without the participation of a Registrar is non-existent, except where the conditions spelled out in §1310 II or III BGB apply, i.e.

– where a person has acted who, though not a Registrar, has publicly exercised the official functions of a Registrar and has entered the marriage in the Marriage Register, §1310 II BGB, or
– where the declarations were not made before the Registrar, but a Registrar has entered the marriage in the Marriage or Family Register and the partners have lived in conjugal community for at least 10 years (5 years if one of them subsequently died), §1310 III No. 2 BGB. For further similar exceptions *cf.* §1310 III No. 2–3 BGB.

87. The declarations have to be given personally, with both of the engaged persons being present at the same time. They may not be made conditionally or subject to a stipulation of time, §1311 BGB. A violation of §1311 BGB will lead to the marriage being 'voidable', i.e. dissolvable with *ex nunc* effect, §1314 I BGB. This does not include situations in which no declaration is given at all; in this case the marriage is non-existent. On the other hand, purely inner or prior reservations that did not become obvious in the declaration will not affect its validity.[1] After the fiancées have made their declarations, the Registrar proclaims in the name of the law that they are now legally united in wedlock. Afterwards, the Registrar shall record the celebration of the marriage in the Family Register, §1312 II BGB.

   1. But *see infra* No. 73 *sqq.*

§4. Effects of Marriage

88. Unlike cohabitation marriage constitutes a legal status and brings about an extensive set of rights and duties which mutually bind the spouses. These duties and rights are based on the idea of conjugal community as spelled out in §1353 I 1 BGB: Marriage is thus concluded for life. This does not preclude the possibility of divorce, but proclaims that marriage may not be dissolved at will and that the effects of marriage may well continue after divorce (e.g. continuing duty to maintain).

I. Duty of Consortium

89. According to §1353 I 2 BGB the spouses are mutually obliged to live in conjugal community – though the legal enforceability in this respect is limited[1] – and they are responsible for each other. Further than that – and in contrast e.g. to the minutely set out maintenance duties – the Code refrains from any further definition of the 'conjugal community' in which the spouses shall live.

The Courts have interpreted conjugal community as a '*consortium omnis vitae*', relating to many aspects of the spouses' life, including where possible the setting up of a joint home, the duty to marital fidelity and to the joint care for common tasks as the household or the upbringing of children.[2] It further includes permission for the other spouse to make use of household effects, except for those effects destined exclusively for the personal use of one of the spouses. On moving in together joint possession of household effects will occur irrespective of ownership.[3]

Joint possession will also arise in relation to the matrimonial home, again irrespective of ownership or tenancy agreements.[4] The right to joint use and joint possession will continue until the spouses separate and one of them accordingly moves out or until the Family Law Court judge accords sole use to one of the spouses.

　1.　*Cf.* §888 Civil Procedure Act (ZPO).
　2.　BGH JZ 1960, 371.
　3.　BGHZ 12, 380.
　4.　BGHZ 71, 216, 223.

90. In marriage, the spouses will be expected to lend each other mutual support and respect.[1] This may become legally relevant in a variety of issues, e.g. when a spouse may follow a chosen career path contrary to the other spouse's wishes. Here, conjugal community has been understood as granting a right of information to the other spouse.

Under the doctrine of equality,[2] marriage is understood as a partnership of equals. No spouse's point of view will thus be given priority in a legal dispute. Courts do not hold jurisdiction over disputes between spouses other than in specially set out instances, e.g. in questions relating to parental care. As opposed to in the past, the Code today refrains from setting out models for the division of the spouses' respective tasks and leaves this to the partners' discretion.

§1356 BGB merely sets out that the management of the household is arranged between the spouses by mutual agreement.[3] If the management of the household is left to one of the spouses, he alone then is in charge of this management. Such internal agreements are not without legal effect, as it defines what is expected of each spouse. This may gain importance in the context of §1579 BGB in divorce proceedings when it has to be decided whether or not a spouse has severely violated the conjugal community as agreed upon by the partners.

1. *Cf.* BGHSt 2, 150, BGH FamRZ 1990, 846, BGH NJW 1954, 1818 for further examples.
2. Art. 3 GG.
3. *Cf.* BGH FamRZ 1960, 21.

91. §1356 II BGB spells out the right of both spouses to be gainfully employed. In the choice and pursuit of this occupation each shall give proper consideration to the interest of the other spouse and the family. A legal duty to work in the profession or business of the other spouse does not exist safe in exceptional circumstances, e.g. under §1360 S.1 BGB if such work constitutes the sole means of safeguarding the familial income or under §1356 II 2 BGB if it were required as proper consideration.

Where such co-operation has been provided by one spouse problems may arise as to the remuneration due for the work.[1] This will be especially relevant when the couple divorces. The ways found by the Courts to deal with the (often common) lack of express arrangements are varied and complicated, using e.g. ideas drawn from corporate law.[2]

1. *Cf.* BVerfG 13, 290; BGH NJW 1995, 3383.
2 E.g. 'Ehegatteninnengesellschaft', *cf.* BGH FamRZ 1975, 35; BGH FamRZ 1990, 973 and 1219.

II. Enforcing Marital Duties

92. The extent to which the marital duties outlined *supra* should be legally enforceable poses difficult questions. Modern law tries to strike a balance by separating out on the one hand essentially 'personal' duties – e.g. the duty to live in marital community – and on the other hand 'economical' duties – e.g. the duty to maintain.

As far as 'personal' duties are concerned, the spouse may bring an action before the Family Law Court claiming the violation of these duties and asking for their fulfilment, e.g. that the other spouse continues to live in marital community or fidelity.[1] Owing to the personal nature of such a claim, even though a court order may be made stating the violation of the duty, such an order will not be legally enforceable.[2] It may still serve as an appeal to the other spouse's co-operation, though, and furthermore may carry indirect consequences under divorce law as proof of the violation of marital duties by the other spouse.[3]

Duties of an 'economical' order, on the other hand, will indeed be enforceable before the Courts. Those include maintenance claims or duties under §1353 I 2 BGB as the right to joint use of the matrimonial home.[4] If applicable, claims may also be made under the general rules of the law of torts (§§832ff, 1004 BGB etc.). Where such 'economical' or general duties have been violated, it is disputed to what extent claims for damages, removal or injunction can be successful without interfering with the special nature of the conjugal community. Claims based on the violation of general rules as in §§823, 1004 BGB will be successful, where absolute personal rights are concerned, e.g. the right to bodily integrity, the right of name or the right to privacy[5] or dignity.

1.   By way of the 'Herstellungsklage'.
2.   §888 III ZPO.
3.   *Cf.* §§1565 II, 1579 Nos. 2–6, 1587c, 1381 BGB.
4.   *Cf.* BGH FamRZ 1988, 143.
5.   BGH FamRZ 1990, 846.

93. Courts have furthermore recognized the matrimonial home as a specially protected sphere[1] the violation of which – e.g. a lover moving into the matrimonial home – may lead to compensatory claims under §§823, 1004 BGB against the other spouse or the third party responsible for the violation.[2]

1.   'Räumlich-gegenständlicher Bereich der Ehe'.
2.   *Cf.* BGHZ 6, 360.

94. Where damages are claimed from the other spouse on whichever ground[1] a limitation of liability applies, §1359 BGB. Spouses are thus answerable to each other in the discharge of the obligations arising out of the marital relationship only for such care as they are accustomed to exercise in their own affairs. In this context §277 BGB spells out that such limitation does not derogate from responsibility for gross negligence.

Possible claims against third parties for violation of the conjugal community *other* than those based on infringement of the matrimonial home have been widely discussed but are not generally awarded by the Courts. The BGH recognizes a right to undisturbed conjugal community,[2] but this is seen as an essential private matter of the spouses that does not bear interference by the state other than that related to the protection of its outer sphere, the matrimonial home.

1.   E.g. §§1360a III, 1613 BGB.
2.   BGH FamRZ 1973, 295.

III. Duty to Maintain

95. The spouses are mutually obliged to support the family adequately, §1360 S.1 BGB. This obligation is characterized by a strongly 'personal' element and by special consideration for the individual standard of living. The rules relating to maintenance among relatives (§§1601ff) are not applicable safe where this is expressly provided for.[1]

The spouses are obliged to apply all means at their disposal to the other spouse's and their minor children's maintenance, §1603 II BGB. This support has to come from both property or work, if property alone cannot safeguard the family income. In cases of need the spouse will be required to take up any form of lawful work to fulfil his obligation to support. Where the management of the household is entrusted to one of the spouses, his obligation to contribute to the support of the family from his work is as a rule fulfilled by the managing of the household.[2]

1. E.g. §1360a III BGB.
2. *Cf.* BGH NJW 1957, 537.

96. The extent of the obligation to support includes all that is required according to the circumstances of the spouses and their children. Both household expenses and personal needs of the spouses and the children have to be provided for, §§1360, 1360a I BGB.[1] Means required for joint support of the family are to be made available for a reasonable period in advance, §1360 II 2 BGB – a provision of importance especially where only one of the spouses has a regular income. It is important to note that future claims for maintenance may not be waived, §1614 I, 1360a III BGB. Also, if a spouse contributes more to the support of the family than he is obliged to give, it will be presumed in case of doubt that he did not intend to demand restitution of such contributions, §1360b BGB.

1. For examples *see* BGH FamRZ 1960, 225; BGH FamRZ 1985, 353.

IV. Transactions for the Provision of Necessities ('Schlüsselgewalt')

A. *General*

97. §1357 BGB sets out special legal consequences for transactions made by one of the spouses for the provision of necessities of life for the family. Where one of the spouses enters into such transactions they are also effective as to the absent spouse. Both spouses thus acquire rights and obligations arising from the transaction.

Historically, the provision was introduced to enable the housewife to manage the household independently, but also to protect creditors by providing that the husband became liable, too, for any contracts entered into by his wife. Since the *First Reform Act on Marriage and the Family 1976*,[1] §1357 BGB applies to both spouses irrespective of who actually manages the household. A transaction will thus also bind the other spouse:

– if it concerns the appropriate provision of the necessities of life for the family,
– if circumstances do not indicate a different conclusion,
– if the spouses are not separated, *cf.* §1567 I BGB,
– and if the spouses have not agreed to limit or exclude the consequences arising from 1357 BGB in a marriage contract and this fact is known to the third party or has been registered according to §1412 BGB.

1. Eherechtsreformgesetz (1. EheRG).

98. There has been (and still is) much dispute as to the definition of a transaction within the meaning of §1357 BGB. To give just a brief outline of points widely agreed upon: §1357 BGB is only concerned with those transactions that are closely connected to familial every-day consuming,[1] e.g. the provision of food and clothing or the purchase of household goods. Excluded are therefore transactions which will fundamentally affect or change the family's living conditions.[2] Here, a spouse may

not act alone with the power to bind the other, but both spouses have to act jointly if both should be legally bound by the transactions.

§1357 BGB does thus not cover e.g. the purchase of land or the termination of the lease for the matrimonial home. Transactions relating to the administration of property or to a spouse's professional career are likewise excluded. Medical treatment[3] will be covered where the couple's children are concerned and §1357 BGB may also apply to treatment received by a spouse (meaning that the other spouse will be liable to cover the costs) where such treatment seems adequate.

The 'family' is understood to comprise the spouses and those of their children who are entitled to support. Provisions will be deemed 'appropriate' if the expenses actually made would seem adequate for an average family of comparable income and standard of living. Where transactions involve the use of credit they will only be appropriate within the meaning of §1357 BGB if the obligations entered into do not burden the household's budget unduly.

1.   *Cf.* e.g. BGH FamRZ 1985, 576.
2.   E.g. in BGH FamRZ 1989, 35.
3.   *Cf.* BGHZ 47, 75, 81.

B. Effects

99.   Where a transaction as envisaged in §1357 BGB is concluded, it will automatically be effective as to the other spouse by law, irrespective of the parties' knowledge of the marital status or intent, unless they agree otherwise. Both spouses are liable for obligations arising from a contract thus concluded as joint debtors (§421 BGB). Likewise, they are both entitled to enjoy the rights stemming from the transaction.

How far §1357 BGB will also cover the dispositions necessary to fulfil the obligations incurred ('Verfügungsgeschäft') is also a matter of dispute. The Federal Supreme Court (BGH) denies such further effect.[1] In practice, this leads to the curious result that – as under German law obligation and disposition are two separate transactions – a husband may on the one hand be liable for the purchase price, but on the other hand may only ask for transfer of ownership to his wife, but not to himself. §1357 BGB is thus reduced to function primarily in protection of creditors.

1.   BGH FamRZ 1991, 923.

V. Presumption as to Ownership

100.   Questions of ownership between spouses are determined by both matrimonial property rules and the general provisions of civil law. Under the statutory regime of community of accrued gains[1] the property of husband and wife – whether acquired before or during marriage – does not become joint property. Such joint property may only occur under the general rules where the spouses decide to purchase jointly. Especially where movable property is concerned the question of who actually owns what may often be difficult to answer for third parties as well as the spouses themselves.

§1362 BGB therefore provides a twofold presumption as to ownership in marriage. In favour of the creditors of husband or wife it is presumed that movables in possession of either of the spouses belong to the debtor. This presumption does not apply if the spouses live in separation and the things are in the possession of the spouse who is not the debtor. In respect of particular things intended for the exclusive personal use of either spouse, it is presumed between the spouses and in relation to the creditors, that they belong to the spouse for whose use they were intended.

1.   'Zugewinngemeinschaft' §§1363ff BGB, *cf. infra* No. 296*sqq*.

VI. Taking of Name in Marriage

101. Under German law, special rules exist as to the name a person might lawfully bear. Traditionally, spouses in Germany bear a joint family name (married name). For a long time this was the husband's name only. Today,[1] especially under the influence of rulings by the Federal Constitutional Court (BVerfG),[2] a married couple enjoys considerable choice as to whether they decide on a joint family name at all and if so, in which way, §1355 BGB. A brief outline of the rather complicated and extensive rules and possible variations may suffice here:

1.   Since the Family Name Act ('Familiennamensrechtsgesetz') of 16 December 1993, in force since 1 April 1994.
2.   BVerfG FamRZ 1991, 535.

102. The spouses may choose as joint family name either of their names at birth, §1355 II BGB. This name then will also become the children's family name, §1616 BGB. A name acquired in a previous marriage is not eligible. Also, the spouses may not combine their birth names to form a joint family name.

Such a combination is only possible for the spouse whose name at birth does not become the married name. Here, his name at birth *or* name acquired in a previous marriage may be inserted before or added after the new married name, §1355 IV BGB. This will be a personal name borne by this spouse only and it will not be transferred to any children of the marriage or to the other spouse.

Any choice of name is made by way of declaration made before the Registrar, §1355 IV S.1, II BGB. Should the couple not decide on a joint married name they both retain their names as borne before the marriage, §1355 I 3 BGB.[1] A spouse's name continues unaltered after divorce, §1355 VI BGB. He may, again by way of declaration made before the Registrar, reassume his name at birth or the name he had at the time of the marriage, §1355 V 2 BGB, or declare to insert or add his name at birth.

1.   For the children's name in this case *cf. infra* No. 158.

§5. Void and Voidable Marriages

103. See supra No. 68*sqq*.

Chapter 2. Divorce

104. Under German law, other than by death, a valid marriage can only be dissolved by judicial decision upon the petition of one or both of the spouses, §1564 BGB. The marriage is dissolved as soon as the judgement becomes final. The legal status hitherto existent between the parties ends though they may still be subject to rights and duties under the law of divorce or any contractual provision entered into by them.

§1. GROUNDS

105. The *First Reform Act on Marriage and the Family 1976*[1] based the German law of divorce on the principle of broken marriage, the question of fault is thus no longer considered by the Court except under §§1565 II, 1568 BGB. There is now only one ground for divorce: that the marriage has failed, §1565 BGB. According to the law, such failure is considered to have occurred where the matrimonial community of the spouses no longer exists and there can be no expectation that the spouses will restore it, §1565 I 2 BGB.

The Family Law Court has to analyse the state of the marriage and arrive at a prediction as to the chances of reconciliation.[2] To avoid prying into the inner workings of the marriage, the Code provides two presumptions for failure of marriage. According to §1566 I BGB there is a conclusive presumption for failure of a marriage if the spouses have been separated for a year and both spouses petition for divorce or the opposing party consents to the divorce. According to §1566 II BGB the same presumption will apply when the spouses have been separated for three years.

1. 1. Eherechtsreformgesetz (1. EheRG), in force since 1 January 1977.
2. *Cf.* BGH FamRZ 1979, 285, 287, 422, 1003; BGH FamRZ 1978, 671; BGH NJW 1995, 1082, 1083.

106. Even where irretrievable breakdown of the marriage has been established this will not always suffice for a divorce to be granted:

1. Where divorce is sought under §1565 I 2 BGB and the spouses have been separated for less than a year, the marriage will only be dissolved if the continuation of the marriage would result in unreasonable hardship to the petitioner owing to causes attributable to the other spouse (§1565 II BGB). 'Unreasonable hardship' as understood by the Courts relates to the mere legal tie between the partners.[1] The causes have to lie with the person of the other partner, i.e. in the case of serious matrimonial offences. The majority of Courts holds §1565 II BGB to be applicable in all cases of divorce, i.e. also to divorce by consent.
2. A spouse may have a legitimate interest in the continuance of a marriage even after its irretrievable breakdown. §1568 BGB thus sets out several reasons for which a failed marriage shall not be severed:

- if, and for as long as it is necessary to uphold the marriage for special reasons in the interest of minor children born of the marriage. The interest of the child has to be considered *ex officio* and theoretically may also prevent a divorce by consent.
- or when and for as long as the divorce would result in exceptional hardship to the party opposing the application. The Courts have been applying the provision very cautiously, regarding it as a means of protection from exceptional hardship resulting specifically from the act of divorce.[2]

1. BGH FamRZ 1981, 127.
2. *Cf.* BVerfGE 55, 134, BGH FamRZ 1979, 422.

107. Where the spouses agree on divorce by consent under §1566 I BGB they have to meet further criteria set out in §630 I, III ZPO. The petition for divorce thus has to include concurrent statements in which the spouses agree as to parental care, maintenance for any common children or among each other and on the distribution of household effects and the use of the matrimonial home.

§2. PROCEDURE

108. Special procedural rules apply in divorce.[1] Jurisdiction lies with the Family Law Court.[2] Proceedings are instituted by petition, §622 ZPO, and they are conducted under the inquisitorial, not the adversary system, §616 I ZPO.[3] In divorce proceedings representation by a lawyer is compulsory.[4] Where this is desired by the parties, divorce and ancillary matters may be heard jointly.[5]

1. *See* §§622ff ZPO, 608, 624 III ZPO.
2. §§23a No. 4, 23b I 2 No. 1 GVG, 606 I ZPO.
3. But *see* §§616 II, 613, 617 ZPO.
4. §78 II No. 1 ZPO, *see also* §§625, 90 II ZPO.
5. §623 I 3 ZPO.

§3. EFFECTS

I. Duty to Maintain

A. *General*

109. In principle, upon divorce the spouses are required to support themselves from their own income and assets. But where this is not possible, German law does not follow a strict doctrine of 'clean break', but recognizes the spouses' continuing responsibility for each other even after divorce. §§1570–76 BGB define the conditions under which a divorced spouse may be entitled to maintenance and set out seven different grounds on which maintenance may be claimed from the other spouse.

B. Grounds for Maintenance

1. Child Care, §1570 BGB

110. First, a divorced spouse may demand maintenance from the other for as long and to the extent that he cannot be expected to pursue gainful employment by reason of having to care for or to educate a child common to both (§1570 BGB). The claim can be made irrespective of who enjoys parental care, it is based solely on the factual caring for the child. Whether (part-time) gainful employment may be expected or not depends largely on the children's age. Extensive jurisdiction exists trying to clarify this question in detail.

2. Age, §1571 BGB

111. A divorced spouse may further be entitled to maintenance in so far as he cannot be gainfully employed on account of his age. The relevant date for making the claim is either the divorce (§1571 No. 1 BGB), the completion of the care for a common child (No. 2) or the cessation of the conditions for a maintenance claim pursuant to §§1572 and 1573 BGB.

3. Infirmity, §1572 BGB

112. Further grounds on which maintenance may be claimed are physical or mental sickness or other infirmity or weakness (§1572 BGB), the relevant date for raising the claim being set as *supr*a.

4. Gross Inequity, §1576 BGB

113. If none of the above named grounds apply, a spouse may still be entitled to maintenance under §1576 BGB if he for other serious reasons cannot be expected to work and if a denial of maintenance would seem grossly inequitable taking into account the position of both spouses.

5. Inability to Find Work, §1573 I BGB

114. Even where according to the rules set out in §1570-1572, 1576 BGB a spouse is expected to support himself, he may not be able to secure employment. In this case §1573 I BGB rules that he can still demand maintenance from the other spouse for as long and to such extent as he is unable to secure 'suitable employment'. To define under which circumstances work may be deemed 'suitable' poses some difficulties and the courts have ruled extensively on this point,[1] naming e.g. the spouse's abilities and his level of training as important considerations.

Similar to the conditions set out in §1570, 1571 and §1572 BGB the claim can only be made within a certain time after the divorce. The failure to secure suitable employment must have occurred reasonably soon 'after the divorce' or after the spouse has ceased to receive maintenance on the grounds of §§1570–72 BGB.

Once established, the maintenance may be granted for a limited period only. In deciding for which length of time maintenance payments will be equitable the Courts will consider e.g. the duration of the marriage, the structure of household arrangements or the care for a common child.

1. *Cf.* BGH NJW-RR 1992, 1282.

6. Additional Maintenance, §1573 II BGB

115. Where a spouse is obliged to provide for himself and has indeed secured employment he may still claim (part-time) maintenance, if his own income is not sufficient to support him. Here, he may claim the difference between his actual income and the full maintenance.[1]

1. BVerfGE 57, 361, 389.

7. Education/Retraining, §1575 BGB

116. Lastly, a divorced spouse may claim support to undergo further education or (re-)training in order to secure permanent self-support, if this spouse omitted or interrupted such training by reason of the marriage or where further training seems necessary for the elimination of disadvantages which arose in the context of the marriage. A successful conclusion of the training must be likely. Also, the claim continues only for such time as it customarily takes to complete the training, not taken into account any delays that the marriage itself may cause.

C. Amount of Maintenance

117. The amount of maintenance actually payable in answer to the claim is determined according to three main ideas, i.e. that:

1. maintenance shall include all necessities of life and that;
2. the actual amount shall depend on the marital circumstances.[1] The latter are determined not so much by the individual spending habits of the couple, but rather by the actual income. In relation to higher incomes, though, the Courts take into account that usually part of the income will be invested.
3. Thirdly, 1578 I 2 BGB allows for individual adjustments where the mere assessment according to the marital circumstances would be inequitable. The Courts may thus limit the claim in time and thereafter reduce it to the necessities of life.

1. §1578 I 1, 4 BGB.

D. The Claimant's Lack of Own Means

118. Maintenance may not be demanded for as long and to such an extent as a spouse is able to support himself from his own income and assets, §1577 I BGB, irrespective of the assets' origins. Should a spouse culpably not realize income this will nevertheless (fictitiously) be accounted to him.[1] The claimant is not required, though, to convert his assets, to the extent that such conversion would be uneconomical or inequitable considering the mutual financial circumstances, §1577 III BGB.

1. *Cf.* BGH FamRZ 1981, 539.

E. The Financial Capacity of the Debtor

119. Full maintenance can only be paid if the obliged spouse's income is sufficiently high. His financial capacity therefore places restrictions on the claim established thus far.

As a rule the Courts assume that both parties have an equal right to the available income,[1] but award a small added bonus to the employed spouse. To ensure a certain uniformity in the application of the law the German Courts issue tables[2] and guidelines[3] mirroring the amount of maintenance granted by them.

Should the debtor marry again, complicated questions arise as to the relation of his continuing and his new duties to maintain. §1582 BGB sets out that as a rule the divorced spouse takes precedence over the new spouse, but in the individual case the order of priority may depend on the reason each claim is based upon (§§1567 *sq.* BGB).

1. So called 'Halbteilungsgrundsatz'.
2. E.g. the 'Düsseldorfer Tabelle', for 1999 *see* FamRZ 1999, 766.
3. Called 'Leitlinien' or 'Richtlinien'.

F. Gross Inequity

120. The post-marital duty to maintain often places severe financial restrictions on the obligee. §1579 BGB allows the claim to be denied, reduced or limited in time in so far as burdening the obligee would be grossly inequitable. When making such a ruling the Court will also consider the interest of a common child entrusted to the debtor. To determine when gross inequitability is to be assumed §1579 BGB lists six specific grounds and one general clause. The payment of maintenance may thus be grossly inequitable if:

121. – the marriage was of short duration only (§1579 No. 1 BGB). Such 'short duration' has been accepted by the Courts where the parties have been married for under two or three years. When calculating the duration of the marriage the time during which a claim could be made under §1570 BGB because of the care for a common child is added to the time that the spouses were actually married;

- the person entitled is guilty of a crime or another serious intentional offence[1] against the debtor or his close relatives (§1579 No. 2 BGB);
- the claimant wilfully caused his own destitution (No. 3). Wilfulness here does not necessarily mean intent, so recklessness may suffice;[2]
- the claimant wilfully disregarded important property interests of the debtor (No. 4) or before the separation grossly violated his duty to contribute to the support of the family during a protracted period (No. 5) or
- if the claimant is solely culpable for an obvious serious misconduct against the debtor (No. 6). As such have been viewed serious matrimonial offences but also any behaviour seriously disapproved of by people in general;
- if there is some other serious ground, which is as grave as the grounds mentioned in No. 1 to 6 (No. 7). This has been assumed by the Courts if the claimant cohabits with a new partner after the divorce and a new marriage is purposefully not entered into to safeguard the maintenance claim. The same will be held true if the claimant lives in 'manifested social community' with a new partner ('feste soziale Verbindung') and this new partner is obviously of financial capacity or where the established external appearance of the new partnership makes the continuing claim against the former spouse seem grossly inequitable.

1. *Cf.* §12 Penal Act (Strafgesetzbuch, StGB).
2. *See* BGH FamRZ 1988, 375.

122. Depending on the circumstances, a loss of maintenance claims under §1579 No. 7 BGB may only be temporary, i.e. it may revive if the new partnership ends.[1]

1. BGH FamRZ 1987, 689.

G. *Mode of Payments*

123. The maintenance is to be provided by payments made each month in advance (§1585 I 1, 2 BGB), in case of exceptional necessity whenever it arises (§1585b I, III BGB). If there is serious reason, the person entitled may demand a capital settlement instead of periodic payments.

124. The maintenance claim becomes extinguished:

- where the conditions for the claim cease to apply;[1]
- on the remarriage or death of the person entitled.[2] Upon the death of the debtor, in contrast, the obligation to provide maintenance passes on to his heirs as a liability of the estate (§1586b I BGB);
- on the payment of a lump sum or capital settlement;[3]
- by way of effective waiving of the maintenance claim.

1. But *see* §1573 IV BGB for a possible revival.
2. §1586 I, but *see* §1586a I BGB.
3. *See supra.*

125. According to §1585c BGB the spouses may conclude agreements as to the maintenance obligations for the period after divorce. The claim may even be waived altogether as §1614 I BGB does not apply to maintenance after divorce. Any waiving by way of agreement is limited by §138 BGB, though, e.g. the agreement will be void if it is against public policy or if it exploits the inexperience or the distressed psychological situation of the other party.

II. Equalization of Support ('Pension Splitting')

126. Since the *First Reform Act on Marriage and the Family 1976* the equalization of accrued gains is extended to the equalization of support also, §1587 BGB. As in the case of other accrued gains any expectation or promise of a pension on the grounds of age, disability or incapacity established during the marriage will be equalized upon divorce. The spouse who has the higher pension expectation or prospect is under an obligation to effect the equalization. The claimant is entitled to one half of the difference in value.

127. The rules according to which equalization of support is to be achieved in the individual case are highly complicated and cannot be set out here in detail. Suffice it to say that the legislator has provided two basic models for equalization, one under public law ('öffentlich-rechtlicher Versorgungsausgleich') and one under private law ('schuldrechtlicher Versorgungsausgleich').

Equalization under the rules of public law is regulated in §§1587b *sq.* BGB. The Family Law Court will transfer the claim to half of the difference in value of the pension rights of one spouse to the other spouse. The court thus transfers one spouse's claim to future pension rights in such a way that the receiving spouse gains an own future claim to the transferred pension rights. Details are to be found in §1587b I-III BGB. Where no equalization under public law is possible a contractual equalization of support will be performed according to §1587f BGB.

128. The spouses may depart from the statutory rules governing pension splitting by way of marriage contract up to the full exclusion of pension splitting. Such exclusion will be deemed ineffective, though, when an application for divorce was entered into within one year after the date of the contract (§1408 I BGB). Further, the spouses can conclude an agreement in connection with the divorce (§1587o BGB). This agreement will require notarial authentication or recording in a Court protocol[1] and the approval of the Family Law Court.

1. *Cf.* §127 BGB.

III. Household Effects and the Matrimonial Home

129. The formal termination of the matrimonial consortium as it occurs latest upon divorce brings about the need to divide the household effects and to determine the use of the matrimonial home. Where the parties cannot agree, these issues will be decided by Court order according to the rules set out in the 'Hausratsverordnung', an Act specially issued for this purpose but not incorporated into the BGB. Jurisdiction lies with the Family Law Court.[1] The procedure follows the rules for non-contentional matters (FGG-Verfahren).

1. §§23b I 2 No. 8 GVG, 621 I No.7 ZPO.

130. In the allocation of household items the Courts will not necessarily follow ownership relationships, but will perform distribution according to equity principles:

– Household items owned jointly by the spouses will be divided equitably and expediently, §8 HausratsVO, under the presumption that effects acquired during the marriage are jointly owned.
– Even items owned solely by one of the spouses may be distributed to the other spouse if he needs them and if such distribution is deemed equitable in the circumstances of the case. Usually the Court order will establish the hiring of the item, only as an exception will the Court transfer ownership.
– Similarly, the Court may issue orders relating to the use of the matrimonial home by way of establishing or reshaping existing tenancy agreements, even if ownership remains unchanged.[1]

1. For details *see* §§3–7 Hausrats VO.

§4. SEPARATION

131. Separation causes legal problems similar to the ones arising upon divorce. In the case of divorce under §1566 BGB the law requires the spouses to have lived apart for a period of at least one year. A legal framework for separation is therefore needed and set out in the Code. Separation as defined in §1567 BGB requires objective and subjective elements. The spouses live in separation when there is no household community between them and one of the spouses manifestly refuses to restore it because he rejects the conjugal community.

According to §1567 I 2 BGB the spouses may also live in separation within their conjugal home as often the financial situation will prohibit the setting up of two separate households for any length of time. Such separation within the conjugal home will be acknowledged by the Courts where no joint household exists and any meeting of the spouses finds its reason in the spatial proximity rather than in the personal relations between the spouses.

As the requirement of separation shall not hinder a possible reconciliation between the parties, §1566 II BGB provides that any living together during a short period only for the purpose of reconciliation does not interrupt or stop the running of the periods indicated in §1566 BGB.

132. Legal consequences arising from the spouses' separation resemble those following divorce:

– Parental care is altered on application only, §1671 II, 1684 BGB. Where the parents continue to exercise joint parental care the residing parent is invested with sole charge relating to matters of daily life (§1687 I BGB).
– A spouse can demand from the other reasonable support according to the living standard and the income and property situation of the spouses (§1361 I 1 BGB). Should a spouse till then not have been gainfully employed he can only be required to work for his own support if this can be expected of him having regard to his personal circumstances. Here, the Court will take into account any earlier gainful occupation, the duration of the marriage and the financial circumstances of both spouses (§1361 II BGB). The housewife in particular shall thus be protected from having to find immediate occupation upon separation.

133. §1361 BGB leads to a fundamental shift in the relations between the spouses: in place of the mutual obligation to maintain we now find a unilateral monetary claim for support which e.g. can no longer be fulfilled by the management of the household.[1] The claim established by §1361 BGB is similar, but not identical to the maintenance claim arising after divorce:

– Household effects may be divided by Court order according to §1361a BGB, if the parties cannot agree among themselves, even though ownership relationship remains unaltered. Each of the spouses is entitled to demand the handing over of household items belonging to him. He is, however, also obliged to leave them in the possession of the other spouse for his use to the extent that the latter needs them for the management of the separate household, but only if leaving them seems equitable. Items owned jointly will be divided according to equitable principles by the Court.
– The Court may grant one of the parties the sole use of the marital home or a part thereof, if this is necessary to avoid serious hardship. In deciding the issue, the Court shall also give attention to ownership when making the order. Even though an order made under the provision does not alter ownership relationships but only regulates the use, the Courts regard §1361b BGB as an exception to the normal rules of ownership and accordingly apply the provision only reluctantly, placing special emphasis on the requirement of 'severe hardship'. The ceding spouse may demand compensation for the use in so far as this seems equitable (§1361b II BGB).

1. *Cf.* §1360 S.2 BGB.

Chapter 3. Cohabitation Outside Marriage

§1. Introduction

134. German law does not know specific legislation for the unmarried couple. Recent legislation, e.g. in child law, suggests that legal solutions in some areas might increasingly be sought regardless of the parent's marital status, though. But as the law stands today neither are the rules relating to marriage generally applicable, nor can they be made so by way of drawing analogies. Relevant legal rules are therefore only to be found:

– in some provisions relating to marriage which as an exception have been allowed to apply analogously;
– in general statutory provisions, applicable without the requirement of marriage;
– and in contractual law based on explicit or implicit agreement between the partners.

§2. Rules Relating to Marriage

135. There are some exceptions to the rule that provisions relating to married couples are not applicable to unmarried partners. Firstly, this is different where the law expressly refers to both marriage and cohabitation.[1] It should be noted, though, that the legislative impetus in these cases has generally not been to grant privileges to cohabitants, but rather to avoid discrimination of married couples and thus to protect the institution of marriage following the demands set out in Art. 6 GG.[2]

1. For an example *see* §122 BSHG and *cf.* BVerf FamRZ 1993, 164.
2. *Cf.* BVerfGE 9, 20.

136. Secondly, there are cases in which statutory provisions have indeed been accepted to apply to cohabitants by way of analogy. This has been advocated most strongly in cases where the legislator primarily wanted to acknowledge the impact of close personal relations or of living together. Though not allowing for a general rule, the Courts have indeed recognized cohabitants to fall within the scope e.g. of §1969 BGB, thus entitling the surviving cohabité to thirty days maintenance and use of the communal home after the partner's death.[1]

Also, where a partner moves in with the other and the landlord refuses his permission, the courts have decided to apply §549 BGB by way of analogy. In the case of a long-term relationship the tenant then generally has a right to such permission unless the landlord can invoke special reasons against this.[2]

1. OLG Düsseldorf FamRZ 1983, 274. For the right to enter into the lease *cf.* BGH NJW 1993, 999 and BVerfGE 82, 6.
2. *Cf.* BGH FamRZ 1985, 42; PLG Hamm NJW 1982, 2876, 774.

§3. General Rules of Civil Law

137. The general rules of civil law apply without reservation to unmarried partners as to everyone else. During the relationship each of the partners manages his property independently. No statutory equalization is made upon their separation. In some cases, this may lead to unsatisfactory results, especially where one of the partners has made financial or other contributions which significantly exceed anything provided in return by the other.

The construction of any subsequent claims for equalization for damages meets with considerable legal difficulties, though German law knows a number of provisions under general civil law on which such claims might theoretically be based. Those include the law of gifts, the law of restitution, the mandate or the concept of actual or undisclosed partnership. Their application in the individual case is complex. As a general rule it might be said that the Courts tend to deny compensation where provisions were meant to serve the communal partnership, but they have acknowledged claims where contributions were made for the benefit of one of the partners only.[1]

1. *Cf.* BGH NJW 1997, 3371; BGHZ 77, 58; BGH FamRZ 1992, 408.

§4. Explicit and Implicit Contractual Agreements

138. It is widely accepted today that cohabitants may freely and validly enter into contracts regulating their legal relations. Such contracts will not be deemed to contravene public policy (§138 BGB) except under special conditions. This may be the case e.g. where contractual provisions unduly interfere with a partner's private life or curtail his right to self-determination – as in the case of entering into an obligation to use contraceptive methods or to continue with the relationship – or where such provisions would gravely violate legitimate interests of close family members.

139. In the majority of cases, the partners do not enter into explicit contractual agreements. This does not necessarily mean that no legal relationships exist between them, but, as under the general rules of contract law, there may be implicit contractual agreements between the partners. The courts have been reluctant in acknowledging the existence of such implicit agreements in the individual case. From the BGH's point of view, in the absence of explicit agreements it should generally be assumed that the partners intentionally refrained from setting up a legal framework for their relation and that any provisions made for the benefit of the other or of the partnership is made so without intention of recovery.[1] This is easily acceptable where such provisions are made to the joint benefit of the partners. The case is different, however, where only one partner profits. Here, a recovery will thus only be possible under the general rules of civil law as outlined *supra.*

1. BGH FamRZ 1981, 530.

Chapter 4. Filiation

§1. MOTHER AND FATHER OF A CHILD

I. Mother

140. Prior to the *Child Law Reform Act 1997*,[1] the BGB did not contain a definition of motherhood. In response to modern developments in artificial reproduction the Reform Act now clarifies the situation: from the law's point of view, where a women gives birth to a child, she alone is to be treated as the child's mother, irrespective of the child's genetic origin. The BGB thereby rejects the idea of 'split motherhood'. There is no way to contest motherhood, nor are agreements between the egg-donor and the gestational mother legally valid.

   1. Kindschaftsrechtsreformgesetz (KindRG) of 16 February 1997.

II. Father

141. When ascribing paternity, the law still recognizes differences according to the marital status of a child's parents. §1592 BGB declares a child's father to be the man:

− who was married to the mother at the time of the child's birth; or
− who has formally declared the child to be his; or
− whose paternity has been established by Court order.

These three possibilities are mutually exclusive. Only paternity established according to §1592 No. 1 and 2 BGB can be contested.[1]

   1. *See* §§1599 I, 1600 BGB.

A. Marriage to the Child's Mother

142. If the parents are married at the time of the child's birth, no further act of recognition is necessary or even possible. The BGB still adheres to the Roman law maxim *'pater est quem nuptiae demonstrant'*.[1] The mere possibility of a prospective annulment (with *ex nunc* effect) of the marriage is irrelevant in this respect. This is different where the marriage is non-existing ('Nicht-Ehe'). Here no paternity will be established.

   The relevant moment at which the parents have to be married is the child's birth. The *Child Law Reform Act 1997* abolished the traditional notion of 'legitimacy by subsequent marriage'. The parents' later marriage therefore does not alter the child's status. It does carry importance in another respect though, as the marriage automatically leads to joint parental care of the spouses (§1626a I No. 2 BGB), even where there had been sole parental care of the mother before (§1626a II BGB)

1. Digest 2, 4, 5.

143. No paternity is attributed where the child is born after the marriage was annulled (with *ex nunc* effect) or after the parent's divorce, even if it was conceived during the time of the marriage. The rationale behind this is that close to divorce or annulment the husband is no longer seen as the child's most probable father. His paternity can only be established by way of Court order or if he officially recognizes the child to be his (§1592 Nos. 2 and 3 BGB).

The situation is different where the marriage has ended through the death of the husband. Here, the law sees no reason to doubt the husband's paternity. Any child born to the widow up to 300 days after the husband's death is therefore legally considered to be his (§§1593 S.2, 1592 No.1 BGB). Where proven, even a longer period of gestation can be recognized (§1593 S.2 BGB).

144. In yet another case does the law depart from the rule that marriage at the time of the child's birth is decisive for the question of paternity: If a child is born during divorce proceedings and another man than the husband formally declares the child to be his, he may be recognized as the father if the husband consents (§1599 II S.2 BGB). The formal declaration can be given prior to the child's birth, though it only gains validity when the marriage is actually dissolved.[1]

1. *See* §§1599 II 1 2.Hs, 1594 IV, 1599 II S.3 BGB.

B. Declaration of Paternity

145. In the absence of already established paternity, a man who is not married to the mother at the time of the child's birth may be recognized as his father if he formally declares the child to be his.[1]

To be valid, this declaration of paternity must be officially recorded by a notary (§1597 I BGB). It can only be given personally (§1596 III BGB). According to §1595 I BGB, the child's mother must consent to the declaration (§1595 I BGB); the same formal requirements apply (§1595–97 BGB). Should she refuse, paternity can only be established by way of Court order (§1592 No. 3 BGB).

Even under the new law, the child's consent is only additionally required where the mother does not have parental care (§1595 II BGB). It has been criticized that the law treats the child as a mere object, whose status may be determined by the mother and the prospective father at their will.

1. §§1592 No.1, 1594–98 BGB.

146. The moment the required declarations have been formally given, paternity is established with all the resulting consequences. No act of Court or public authority is necessary. The father will be recorded in the register of birth, though this is no requirement to the validity of the declaration. The effect is *ex nunc* only (§1594 BGB), with an exception in the area of maintenance duties.[1]

    1. *Cf.* §1613 II No. 2 BGB, *see infra* No. 267*sqq.*

C. Contesting Paternity

147. Paternity – whether established by marriage bond or by official declaration – may be contested by bringing an action before the Family Law Court.[1]

The child, the child's mother and the man till then recognized to be the father by way of marriage or official declaration are allowed to bring the action (§1600 BGB). Now neither the genetic father nor – as had been the case under the old law – the deceased husband's parents or any other relatives are granted the right to contest paternity. The question of who should be invested with the right to bring such an action was highly debated during the legislative process; the present reform is unlikely to put an end to the dispute.

    1. For the procedure *see* §§23 I S.2 No. 12 GVG, X 640 II No. 3 ZPO, §1600e I BGB.

148. The father wishing to terminate this status must bring proceedings against the child (§1600e I BGB). If the action is brought by the mother or the child it must be directed against the father. Proceedings are instituted by bringing an action against the other party. If the relevant party has died, proceedings may still be instituted despite the absence of a respondent (with important consequences e.g. in the area of succession).

Where the child is contesting paternity, problems may arise if the child has not yet come of age. According to §1600a II BGB it is the legal representative who then conducts the proceedings. §1600a IV BGB provides that the legal representative may only bring an action if this is in the best interest of the child.

149. It is important to note that paternity can only be contested within two years from the time at which the contestant becomes acquainted with the relevant facts leading to the challenge (§1600b I 1, II BGB). This period shall start no earlier than the birth of the child and the coming into effect of a declaration of paternity (§1600b II 1 BGB).

A special rule applies where the child is contesting paternity: even if the legal representative has allowed the two year period to expire this does not preclude the child from lodging an action on his own account after his coming of age. The relevant moment in determining the expiry of the two year period then becomes the child's own knowledge of the relevant facts, starting no earlier than the child's coming of age (§1600b III BGB). Even after the two years have passed the child may contest paternity where special circumstances have arisen that would render remaining under the current status intolerable for the child (§1600b V BGB).

150. An action answering to the formal requirements named *supra* will be successful if the Court considers the claim made to be legally justified. The Court must be convinced that the man to whom till then paternity was ascribed is in fact not the child's genetic father. The burden of proof lies fully with the contesting party, which must rebut the law's presumptions spelled out in §1592 No. 1 and 2 BGB. The action is a purely negative one. It is thus not necessary to establish who indeed is the child's genetic father – though this may be the subject of subsequent paternity proceedings.

The successful Court action is brought to an end by the *ex tunc* termination of the paternal relationship by order of the Court, dating back to the time of its coming into existence (e.g. the birth of the child in the case of paternity by way of marriage). The Court's decision is binding on everyone, not just *inter partes*.[1] Previously granted maintenance for the child becomes groundless. Past claims under an intestacy now lack legal justification as well as nationality exclusively ascribed to the child by paternity: The child attains the status it would have held without the successfully contested paternity ever coming into existence.

   1. §640h I S.1 ZPO.

151. Where paternity is successfully contested, the previous 'father' often has been maintaining the child presumed to be his for years. Recovery of those payments from the child under the law of restitution will rarely be possible, as §818 III BGB prohibits repayments where the money has actually been spent. §§1613 II No. 2a, 1607 III 2 BGB therefore lifts the ban prohibiting maintenance claims for the past and allows the previous father to recourse to the actual father – once he has been established as such.

Damages claims against the mother will only succeed in exceptional circumstances, though, e.g. where the mother has wilfully used an alleged paternity to achieve marriage or hinder an action of contest.[1]

   1. BGH FamRZ 1990, 367, 369.

D. *Establishing Paternity by Judicial Decision*

152. In the absence of valid paternity by way of marriage or official declaration, or where such paternity has been successfully contested, a person may appeal to the Court to establish paternity (§1600d I BGB). Actions may only be brought by:

–   a prospective father against the child;
–   the child against the man presumed to be its father;
–   the child's mother against this man.

Exclusive jurisdiction lies with the Family Law Court.[1]

The application is successful if the man in question is indeed the child's genetic father, whether by procreation or sperm donation. The Court will inquire into the matter *ex officio*.[2] The truth of the proposition is proven to the satisfaction of the Court if all evidence and circumstances point with near certainty to the alleged father.

   1. §23 I 2 No.12 GVG, §§621 I No. 1, 640 II No. 10 ZPO.
   2. §§ 640 I Hs.2 with 616 I ZPO.

153. Faced with the difficulties of proving genetic descent, the law works with the presumption that paternity can normally be inferred from the fact that a man had sexual intercourse with the mother about the time when the child was conceived (§1600d II 1 BGB). The statutory period of conception runs from 181 to 300 days before the date of the child's birth – unless a different time-span is proven (§1600d III 2 BGB). Intercourse during the time has to be established. The presumption can be rebutted by evidence establishing serious doubts as to the man's paternity (§1600 II 2 BGB). It is also possible to obtain a negative declaration of paternity,[1] sole jurisdiction again lies with the Family Law Court.

The Court's declaration again is binding on everyone.[2] All claims regarding the parent-child relationship – e.g. maintenance claims – can rely on the Courts decision once it has come into existence, even claims concerning the past (§1600d IV BGB).

1. §640 II No. 1 ZPO.
2. §640 I S.1, 3 ZPO.

E. Artificial Reproduction

154. Artificial reproduction as such is not generally prohibited under German law. The *Protection of Embryos Act 1990*[1] places restrictions on some techniques classified as abusive. Under the new law, artificial reproduction is not considered when determining who the child's legal mother is: it is the birth-mother alone who is recognized as the mother, whether she is indeed the child's genetic mother or not. Maternity thus established cannot be challenged under German law.[2] Agreements between the genetic and the gestational mother as to a transfer of the child to the genetic mother or any other woman are prohibited and legally void.

1. Embryonenschutzgesetz.
2. *See supra* No. 140.

155. The situation is different where the father is concerned. Here the genetic father – even if acting as sperm donor only – may attain the status as the child's father by way of the proceedings presented *supra*. It is problematic though, whether the husband who previously agreed to his wife's heterologues artificial insemination should subsequently be allowed to contest his paternity (§1591 No. 1 BGB). The Federal Court of Justice follows the opinion that such prior consent does not preclude the right later to contest the paternity, which it holds to be an unalienable right.[1]

In the majority of cases, the Court also does not see a violation of the principle of '*venire contra factum proprium*' as pointed out by scholars and other Courts. On the other hand, the Federal Court of Justice has ruled that the husband's consent to his wife's treatment is to be interpreted as a contract for the benefit of a third party, namely the child. The husband is thereby in all events bound to maintain a child thus born – an obligation that will continue even after he successfully contests his paternity.

1. BGHZ 87, 169; BGH NJW 1995, 2921.

156. The legal position of the sperm donor results directly from the rules outlined *supra*: where no other man is recognized as the child's legal father or where such paternity has been successfully contested, he may officially declare the child to be his or seek a Court order to such effect (§1592 No. 2, 3 BGB).

In most cases, though, the sperm donor will be more interested in safeguarding his anonymity. Here, German law provides little protection.[1] Once he has been established as the child's genetic father, he is under the same legal obligations – e.g. to maintain the child – as every father. The mother may not renounce such claims on behalf of the child (§1614 I BGB).

  1.   *See infra* No. 157.

III. Knowledge of One's Genetic Origins

157. The Federal Constitutional Court has deducted a right to know of one's genetic origins from the German constitution, Art. 2 I, 1 I GG.[1] The *Child Law Reform Act 1997*[2] has substantially increased the child's rights to contest and establish paternity. This does not apply to maternity, though. As it also severs the tie to the previous father it is seen by critics as too radical a way for a child just searching for its genetic origin. On the basis of §242 and §1618a BGB Courts have also been known to allow the child to bring an action against its mother to disclose information about the genetic father. The issue is a difficult one, though, as the Courts are dealing with conflicting fundamental rights protected under the constitution: the child's right to know of its genetic origin versus the mothers right to privacy.

  1.   BVerfGE 79, 256.
  2.   Kindschaftsrechtsreformgesetz (KindRG) of 16 February 1997.

§2.   THE POSITION OF THE CHILD (GENERAL)

I. The Child's Name

158. German law knows a set of intricate rules regulating the use of a name. Parents thus enjoy only limited freedom where the child's name is concerned. They may choose the child's first name, but only as long as the child's welfare is not jeopardized by the choice. Registration of the name will thus be refused e.g. where the child would be subject to ridicule because of the name chosen. If the parents cannot agree on a first name for the child, the dispute will be solved by the Courts (§1628 BGB).

159. Complicated rules govern the child's last name: Where the child's parents are married and have decided on a common family name (§1355 I 1, II BGB), the child will automatically be given this same name. Where the spouses do not bear the same name (§1355 I 3 BGB), they may decide on either of their surnames as the child's last name. This decision then will be binding for any prospective children as well (§1617 I 3 BGB).

160. As the right to choose the child's surname springs from parental care, similar rules apply where the parents are not married, but have given a declaration of joint parental care.[1] Should the parents not agree on the child's surname within one month of his birth, the Registrar will notify the Court.[2] The Court then grants the right to determine the name to one of the parents (§1617 II 4 BGB).

In the case of sole custody exercised by one of the parents who is not married, the child will bear this parent's name (§1617a I BGB). Where both parents agree – as well as the child if he is older than five years of age, §1617a II 2 BGB) – the child may also be named after the non-custodial parent (§§1617e II 1; 1617a III 3, 4; 1617c I BGB).

> 1. Following the rules set out in §§1594 IV, 1626b II BGB.
> 2. §21 Law on Civil Status ('Personenstandsgesetz' PStG).

161. Later changes to the child's last name can only be effected by special circumstances, as e.g. the parents' subsequent decision to take on a common family name (§1355 III, 1617c I BGB) or to agree on joint parental care (§1617b II BGB), or where one or both of the custodial parents (re-)marry (§1617c II BGB). The law also provides the possibility to change a child's last name if it has been established that his father is not his genetic parent, §1617b II BGB.

II. Assistance and Due Consideration

162. §1618a BGB spells out a general rule for the relationship between parent and child: they owe each other assistance and due consideration. Though this provision may not in itself be the basis for claims between children and parents it has to be borne in mind where the interpretation of legal rights and duties within the family is concerned. Thus e.g. maintenance claims may be forfeited by a given violation of §1618a BGB.[1] The Courts have also used the principle to limit liabilities of children (already of age) who undertook to guarantee for their parent's debts if the parents secured such guarantee in violation of the principle of assistance and due consideration and if the creditor exploited such violation.[2]

> 1. Doctrine of 'Rechtsmißbrauch' (abuse of rights).
> 2. *See* BGH NJW 1994, 1341; 1997, 52.

Chapter 5. Adoption

§1. APPLICATION AND CONSENT

163. Under German law, adoption is performed by Court order made at the application of the prospective parent(s) (§1752 BGB) and with the consent of a number of specified parties.

The initiative lies with the adoptive parent(s). The application has to be officially recorded and can only be made personally, unconditionally and unlimited in time, §1752 II BGB. The applicant will have to have reached the age of twenty-five. Twenty-two years of age will suffice in the case of in-family adoptions or where the applicants are married and the other spouse has reached the age of twenty-five, §1743 S.1, 2 BGB.

164. As a rule, spouses may only apply jointly for an adoption order to be made (§1741 II 2, 1754 I BGB), unless one of them is the child's natural parent (*see* §1741 II 4 BGB for further exceptions). Unmarried persons, in contrast, may only adopt on their own, §1741 II 1 BGB. German law does not know joint adoption by an unmarried couple. Except where a spouse joins a previous adoption made by the partner before the marriage, a child may only be adopted once during the lifetime of the adopters, §§1742 BGB.

165. The prior consent of the following people is required before an adoption order will be made:

a) The child: Where the child is under fourteen years old, the legal representative will act for the child, §1746 I 2 BGB. Where the child has reached fourteen years of age and enjoys limited legal capacity, the child has to act himself, though with the legal representative's approval.
b) The child's natural parents: Their consent is needed irrespective of their marital status and of whether they are vested with parental care or not, §1747 BGB. To ensure the natural parent's freedom of decision the law provides that their consent may not validly be given until eight weeks after the child's birth. This is different only in the case of the unmarried father, who may consent even prior to the child's birth, §1747 III 1 BGB. Once granted, the consent is irrevocable. It will lose its validity, though, where the application for the adoption order is refused or withdrawn or where no order is made during the following three years.

Under exceptional circumstances, the natural parents' consent may be dispensed with by the Court, e.g. where a parent's residence is unknown. The Court can also substitute the parent's consent where severe danger to the child's welfare is at stake. This intrusion into the very element of parental rights requires a serious violation of parental duties as spelled out in §1748 I BGB, e.g. major crimes against the child.

c) The adoptive parent's spouse and the child's spouse: In the first case only, the unwilling spouse's consent may be substituted by the Court unless his/her refusal is based on legitimate conflicting interests, §1749 I 2,3 BGB.

§2. Placement Prior to Adoption

166. The adoption order shall only be made where the child has already been placed with the prospective adopter for a reasonable amount of time, §1744 BGB. §1751 BGB provides a legal framework for such placement prior to adoption: From the natural parents' consent onwards, their parental care and the right to have contact with the child are suspended.

The local Youth Welfare Authority will act as guardian. The prospective adopters gain the right to decide on matters of daily life and to represent the child legally thus far, §§1751 I 5, 1688 I BGB. They furthermore become liable for the child's maintenance, §1751 IV BGB.

§3. The Adoption Order and its Effects

167. Jurisdiction for the issue of adoption orders lies with the Guardianship Court.[1] Where the legal requirements described *supra* have been met with, the Court will grant the order if this is beneficial to the child's welfare and if it can be expected that a true parent-child relationship will develop between the parties. §1741 I, 1745 BGB states that financial interests should not be decisive. Once made, the order is unappealable and irrevocable.[2]

    1. 'Vormundschaftsgericht' (VormG).
    2. But *see infra* No. 170, 171.

168. No adoption order may be granted posthumously for the deceased child, §1753 I BGB. Adoption after the death of the prospective adopter, on the other hand, is possible, provided he had already lodged the application or had arranged with a notary for the lodging. An adoption order then granted will have retroactive effect, dating back to the applicant's death, §1753 III. It will thus be possible for the adopted child to claim statutory rights of inheritance.

169. Once the order comes into effect the adopted child gains the full legal position as the adopters' offspring and becomes a member of their families. This includes all statutory rights to inheritance, maintenance etc. in relation to the new family. At the same time, the ties to the child's natural parents and their family are severed, §1755 BGB.

The child's name changes upon adoption and becomes the adoptive parents' family name, §1757 I BGB. On application and with the child's consent, the Court may grant leave to the child to bear both the old and new family name in any order, §1757 IV S.2 No.2 BGB.

§4. Revocation of the Adoption Order

170. As a rule, an adoption order once granted is irrevocable and final so as to provide a stable basis for the new family. Under exceptional circumstances mentioned in the Code the law departs from this course and allows for a revocation. This is the case where the required declarations were not or not validly given[1] or where a fundamental error in making such a declaration has occurred.[2]

Any such defects, though, are remedied three years after the adoption order has come into effect, §1762 II 1 BGB. Furthermore, even before that time there is a ban on revocation if this would seriously jeopardize the child's welfare and the Court sees no overriding interest on the side of the adopters, §1761 II BGB.

1. E.g. lack of valid application, or of a required consent, *see* §1747, 1746 BGB.
2. E.g. mistake as to the child's identity or duress, *see* §1760 II BGB.

171. The revocation of an adoption order does not have retroactive effect, §1764 I 1 BGB. Once the revocation order has become non-appealable the family ties previously established by the adoption come to an end and those then severed revive, §§1764 II, III BGB. The natural parents do not automatically regain parental care, but will be granted such by the Court unless this should be contrary to the child's welfare, §1764 IV BGB.

Chapter 6. Parental Care

§1. ACQUIRING PARENTAL CARE

172. As a rule, parental care ('elterliche Sorge') – meaning all the duties and rights of a parent in relation to his/her child – is attributed to both parents alike. Under certain conditions German law also knows sole parental care. Even then the tie between the other parent and the child is not completely severed, though, and some rights and duties (e.g. duty to maintain, right to contact) remain. Parental care may be acquired in a threefold way: automatically by law, by declaration and by Court order.

I. Parental Care Acquired by Law

173. Where the parents are married at the birth of the child, both acquire parental care automatically without any further act being required or even possible.[1] Parental care thus acquired continues until ended by law (e.g. at the death of the parent) or by Court order. The parents' divorce or separation thus remains without influence on the continuing parental care for the child. Where the parents are not (yet) married at the time of the child's birth – and have not given a declaration of joint parental care –, only the mother has parental care, §1626a BGB. Subsequent marriage of the parents will lead to automatic joint parental care though – comparable to the idea of legitimization by subsequent marriage under the old law.

  1. *Cf.* §1626a BGB.

II. Parental Care Acquired by Formal Declaration

174. Where the parents are not married to each other at the time of the child's birth joint parental care can also result form a formal declaration. This declaration is only effective if made in the prescribed form: It has to be given by both partners personally and unconditionally (§1626b I BGB) and it has to be officially recorded.[1] It is not possible to limit the extent to which one or both of the partners will exercise parental care.

The declaration becomes legally effective only when validly made by both parents and after the child has actually been born – even though it is possible to lodge a declaration prior to the birth, §1626b II BGB. There is no time-limit as to when the declaration has to be made other than the child's coming of age. Where parental care over a child has already been determined by a Court order, there is no room for any declarations of parental care, §1626b III BGB.

As long as the requirements as spelled out in §§1626a–d BGB are adhered to, the declaration will be valid. Even a violation of general rules – e.g. in the case of fraudulent misrepresentation – will not render the declarations invalid.

1.   §§1626d I BGB, 59 I 1 No. 8 SGB VIII.

175. The parents' declarations do not have to be given together or simultaneously. They do not form a contract but run parallel to each other, leading to the curious result that the father lodging his declaration might not even know that the child's mother has already done so. Further, it is not necessary that the parents cohabit. In the case of non-cohabitation, joint parental care will be exercised by granting the resident parent the sole right to decide on daily affairs, §1687 I 2,3, BGB.[1]

1.   *See infra* No. 183.

176. At no point in the proceedings is there any inquiry into the child's welfare. But once a declaration of joint parental care has come into effect, the parents' disposition ends: any change as to parental care can now only be brought about by the court order, e.g. under §1666 BGB, if the child's welfare is seriously endangered or on application by one of the parents.

III. Parental Care Acquired by Court Order

177. A parent may only apply for a parental care order when the family situation has altered significantly, e.g. upon the parent's separation, §§1671, 1672 BGB,[1] or where an order granted previously is asked to be changed. When deciding upon making the order, the child's welfare is the first consideration, §1697a BGB.

1.   *Cf.* §§1678 II, 1680 II, III; 1681 II BGB.

§2. PERSONAL CARE (§§1626 I 1, 1631 BGB)

178. Parental care for a child is exercised in two main areas: in the personal and financial sphere. German law thus distinguishes between personal and financial care as the duties of a parent. Personal care grants the parents' rights and duties in relation to the child and to third parties. Its main objective is the furthering of the child's interest and welfare. In the area of personal care – as well as with financial care – the right to legally represent the child (§1629 BGB) plays a key-role.

Parents further have a right to determine the child's residence (§1631 BGB) and a right to physical possession enforceable against anyone who detains the child against the parents' demands (§1632 I BGB). The parents also possess the right to control and direct contact made with the child (§1632 II BGB). §1626 II BGB points out, though, that when providing care and upbringing the parents shall take into account the growing ability of the child and his need to act independently and with a sense of responsibility. Parents shall therefore discuss questions of parental care with the child to the extent that his development indicates and they shall endeavour to act in agreement.

179. Where a child is or has been married the personal care is limited to legal representation (§1633 BGB), whereas financial care continues undiminished.

§3. THE WELFARE PRINCIPLE

180. The guiding principle for a parent exercising parental care shall be the child's welfare. The Basic Law ascribes the right to direct the child's upbringing to the parents;[1] it is thus not primarily for the state to determine how this welfare is best achieved in practice. The state is under an obligation to intervene, though, where the child is suffering or is likely to suffer significant harm.

The law still aims to provide some guidelines as to the meaning of the welfare principle: §1626 II BGB reminds parents to take into account the child's increasing capacity to arrive at decisions of his own and to consult with the child accordingly. This applies especially where the child's education is concerned: §1631a BGB. §1631 II BGB prohibits humiliating treatment of the child. The law especially mentions corporal and spiritual maltreatment, but does not to date generally outlaw corporal punishment of any kind, though this was debated in the legislative process.

   1.   Art. 6 II 2 GG.

§4. LEGAL REPRESENTATION

181. Parents may exercise legal representation for the child in a twofold way: by acting for the child and by consenting to the child's own acts. The child may also be covered by contracts between its parents and third parties by way of the contracts with protective effects *vis-a-vis* third parties.[1]

Legal representation of the child is exercised either jointly by the parents (§1629 I 2 BGB) or by one parent alone (§1629 I 3 BGB), depending on who has parental care for the child.

   1.   The so-called 'Vertrag mit Schutzwirkung zugunsten Dritter'.

I. Joint Parental Care

182. Where the parents share joint parental care, both parents have to act for the child, though representation may be arranged between the parents. If the parents cannot agree the Family Law Court may transfer the right to decide to one of the parents and thus in so far grant sole legal representation (§1628 BGB). Where they cannot agree, the Court may also grant one parent the sole right to decide in a certain field, e.g. where medical treatment is concerned. Furthermore, a parent may always decide alone in the case of imminent danger, provided the other parent is then informed without delay (§1629 I 4 BGB).

183. Upon the parents' separation, the right to decide on daily matters remains solely with the resident parent (§1687 I 1–3 BGB).

II. Limits of Legal Representation

184. German law knows several other instances in which the parent's right to legal representation is curtailed in order to protect the child's interest or to give credit to his growing capacity to arrive at his own conclusions. Here it shall suffice just to highlight some examples:

a) Transactions which seem likely to jeopardize the child's interests will additionally need the consent of the Family Law Court,[1] e.g. the disposal of the child's property (§1821 I No. 1 BGB), of all his assets at once (§1822 No. 1 BGB), when debts are incurred in the child's name (§1822 No. 8 BGB) or the disclaimer of an estate. Here, the Family Law Court decides according to the welfare principle whether or not to grant the parents permission to undergo the transaction in question. (§1697a BGB). But whether or not the parents eventually act on that permission is at their discretion.

b) The law denies the parents the power to decide for the child altogether where a conflict of interests between the child and the parents seems likely, e.g. in the case of legal transactions between the child and one or both of the parents or a close relative (§§ 181, 1795 II, 1795 No. 1 BGB). These restrictions do not apply though, where the transaction as of right might only be beneficial for the child.[2] Should the parents still act for their child, contrary to the prohibitions afore mentioned, they act without power of representation (§§177*sqq.* BGB). Their actions might be sanctioned by the child once it has come of age. Also, the Court may subsequently grant its permission.

c) The Federal Constitutional Court has further decided that these restrictions may not suffice to protect the interest of the child: Parents may thus not enter into obligations which will burden the child with debts to an extent where the aim of enabling the child to lead a self-determined life at reaching majority would be put in danger.[3] Accordingly, the *Act Limiting the Liability of Minors*[4] introduced §1629a BGB, which now limits the child's liability for engagements the parents made for the child (§1629a BGB).

1. *See* §§1643 I, II; 1821f.; 112 BGB.
2. BGHZ 59, 236; BGH FamRZ 1975, 480.
3. BVerfGE 72, 155.
4. 'Gesetz zur Beschränkung der Haftung Minderjähriger' of 1 January 1999.

§5. Disagreement between Holders of Parental Care

185. Where parental care is exercised by both parents, decisions shall be taken jointly and to the welfare of the child, §1627 S. 1, 2 BGB. Disagreements which cannot be resolved by the parents themselves may ultimately be taken before the Family Law Court, §1628 BGB. At the application of at least one of the parents the Court will issue an order if the matter is of considerable importance and a decision is in the interest of the child, 1697a BGB. In granting the order, the Court will transfer the right to one of the parents according to the welfare principle as shown *supra.*[1]

1. *Cf. supra* No. 180.

186. §1628 BGB grants the Court the power to transfer the right to decide all future questions arising in a specific area to one of the parents. As an exception to the idea of joint parental care this should only be granted in special circumstances.

§6. SELF-DETERMINATION OF THE CHILD

187. As the child matures, the scope of parental care diminishes, §1626 II BGB.[1] This recognition of the child's growing maturity is expressed in a number of provisions in the Code:

a) From the age of fourteen the child alone will decide the question of his religious denomination, §5 *Religious Upbringing of Minors Act.*[2]
b) From the age of sixteen onwards the minor can draw up a Will (2247 IV BGB) without the parent's consent being necessary, §2229 II BGB.
c) Consent to medical treatment will depend on the understanding of the child.[3] The conditions under which the child's consent alone will suffice to allow for medical treatment, e.g. an abortion, are still a matter of controversy.
d) The child also enjoys increased procedural rights as he grows older: A minor above the age of fourteen always has to be heard in proceedings relating to his personal care.[4] Younger children will be heard if the Court deems this to be necessary.
e) Also from the age of fourteen onwards the child is entitled to an appeal to a higher court[5] where e.g. a parental care order (§1671 BGB) or a contact order (§1671 BGB) is concerned.

  1. *See supra* No. 178.
  2. 'Gesetz über die religiöse Kindererziehung'.
  3. 'Natürliche Einsichtsfähigkeit', BGHZ 29, 33.
  4. §50b FGG.
  5. *See* §59 I 1, III FGG.

§7. PROTECTION FOR PARENTAL CARE

188. Parental care may need to be protected from undue influences of third parties. The state guarantees the undisturbed exercise of parental care by way of granting the parents certain rights against third parties in §1632 BGB. Parental care is also recognized to be a right protected under the law of torts, §823 I BGB.

I. Possession of the Child

189. According to §1632 BGB the holder of parental care may thus request the return of the child to him of any third party provided this does not run counter to the child's welfare. The right may be exercized against the other parent as well where parental care lies solely with the requesting parent.

II. Contact

190. Parents furthermore have the right to determine who is to contact the child. If necessary, they may apply for a Court order to defend that right whether it is a third party or the child himself who seeks the undesired contact. Where the child is approaching majority this might be problematic in view of the child's growing maturity and right to self-determination, §1626 II BGB.

The Courts here will cautiously weigh the interests at stake and will only on plausible grounds go against the child's express wishes. Courts will be especially careful where a positive relationship has been established even if this happened against the parents' wishes. It should be noted, though, that §1632 II BGB is not applicable where contact between the child and the non-residential parent is concerned.[1]

> 1.   *Cf. infra* No. 217*sqq.*

§8. Third Parties Caring for Children

191. As a rule, parental care is strictly personal and cannot be transferred as a whole to a third party. Parents can only invest others temporarily with certain rights in relation to the child, as e.g. in the case of neighbours caring for the children.

192. The situation is different where the parents are not willing or able to undertake the child's upbringing, but also do not want to free the child for adoption. Foster carers may then be asked to take on the factual role as a parent,[1] while parental care remains vested in the parents. §1688 BGB tries to balance the potentially conflicting interests between parents and foster carers. The Court can thus temporarily transfer certain rights to the foster carers, especially relating to daily affairs, §§1688 I 1, 2, 3; 1629 BGB, though not against the parents express wishes, §1688 III 1 BGB.

> 1.   So-called 'Familienpflege', *cf.* §33 SGB VIII for the financial side of this.

193. Should the parents request the child's return to the detriment of the child's welfare, the Family Law Court may order the child to remain with the foster family, §1632 IV BGB. As this poses a severe curtailment of the constitutionally guaranteed parental right, the child's welfare has to be seriously endangered for the Court to make such an order.

With the parents consent, the Family Law Court may further transfer rights to the foster carers to the exclusion of the parents under §1630 II BGB.

§9. Care for the Child's Property

194. On the financial side, the parents' care shall chiefly aim at the conservation and augmentation of the child's assets. With the exception of the assets named in §1638 BGB, these include everything the child owns and acquires, including anything purchased by the parents with the child's means.[1]

In governing the assets, the parents are bound by the ideas of economic property management, §1642 BGB. Should this be endangered the Family Law Court may intervene, §1667 II BGB. Transactions which are typically potentially dangerous to the integrity of the child's fortune also require the Court's prior consent, §1643 BGB, as the parents' power to represent the child in so far is restricted.[2]

1. Principle of 'surrogation', §1646 BGB.
2. *See supra* No. 184.

195. The Code also outlines how the child's assets shall be used: Income is to be used primarily to cover the cost of administering the property and the cost of maintaining the child, §1649 BGB. The original capital shall only be touched if otherwise the child's maintenance would be jeopardized. Any remaining income shall be invested anew. §1649 II 1 BGB allows for a limited use of surplus income for the maintenance of the parents or of any minor unmarried siblings,[1] based on the idea of family solidarity.

1. Notwithstanding the rules found in §1602 I BGB.

§10. Claims between Parents and Children Arising from the Exercise of Parental Care

196. If the parents incur expenses in the exercise of parental care which they are entitled to consider necessary in the circumstances, they may demand compensation from the child to the extent that they themselves are not chargeable for such expenses (§1648 BGB). Upon the termination of the care the parents have to release the child's property and on demand also have to render an account of its administration (§1698 I BGB).

197. As a rule, parents may also be held liable for a breach of their parental duties. §1664 BGB sets out that parents exercising parental authority shall be responsible only for such care as they customarily apply to their own affairs. But the relation of §1664 BGB to the general rules of tort add thus the exact extent of the parents' liability, is a matter of considerable dispute.[1]

1. *Cf.* e.g. BGH FamRZ 1988, 267.

§11. State Support

198. Parents who for whatever reason encounter difficulties in caring adequately for their children are entitled to rely on the state for assistance and support. This will chiefly be provided by the Family Law Court in the form of orders and also by the local authorities, acting through the local Youth Welfare Office ('Jugendamt'). The Courts may assist by way of admonitions or warnings to the child or by granting orders, e.g. transferring the child to an educational institution of the parents' choice.

Any Court orders will take into account the welfare of the child. On application by the parents, the local Youth Welfare Office will provide 'assistance' ('Beistandschaft') under a special new legal framework as spelled out in §§1712–1717 BGB. They will support holders of parental care in proceedings concerning filiation (§1712 I No. 1 BGB) and maintenance claims (§1712 I No. 2 BGB). Rights arising from parental care are not curtailed by this assistance.

199. On a non-judicial side, the local Youth Welfare Office and the 'Kinder- und Jugendhilfe' will provide help in further areas relating to the upbringing and welfare of children if so requested by the parents.

§12. STATE CONTROL

200. The Basic Law grants the parents the fundamental right to determine the upbringing of their offspring as they think fit.[1] The state nevertheless has to fulfil its role as guardian of the child's own basic rights[2] and may therefore be authorized to curtail parental rights in order to protect children whose carers abuse them or are unable or unwilling to look after them. §1666 BGB enables the Family Law Court to intervene in cases where the welfare of the child or of his assets are endangered.

    1. Art. 6 II GG.
    2. Idea of the 'staatliches Wächteramt'.

I. Personal Welfare

201. The Courts may act to protect children from dangers to their physical, mental or spiritual welfare. To allow for an order under §1666 this danger must result from either:

– abuse of parental care;
– neglect of the child;
– inadvertent behaviour of the holder of parental care; or
– the actions of third parties,

and the parents must be unwilling or unable to avert the danger themselves.

202. The Code does not specify which orders the Court may grant in reaction to such circumstances. The judge enjoys discretion to make the appropriate orders to keep the child from harm. These may range from placing the child under institutional or foster care to ultimately withdraw parental care altogether from the parents. The Court may also substitute the parent's consent where necessary, e.g. to medical treatment of the child.

Only such orders may be made which follow the principle of reasonableness and which are proportionate to the impending danger, as is pointed out in §§1666a I, II BGB. Orders may be altered by the Court at any time (§1696 BGB) and the Court is under an obligation to do so whenever the danger to the child's welfare ceases to be imminent.[1]

    1.   *Cf.* S1696 II, III BGB.

II. Management of Financial Affairs

203. §1666 BGB also grants the Court powers over the child's assets where those are put into jeopardy by abuse of parental care, neglect, inadvertent behaviour of the parents or the conduct of third parties. The child's financial interests are endangered if the parents act blatantly contrary to economic principles or from motives of self-interest and thus risk diminishing or loss of the child's fortune or his indebtedness, *cf.* also §1666 II BGB. Again, the Court enjoys wide discretion in the orders it will make while it is bound by the principle of proportionality.

§13. CHANGE IN PARENTAL CARE

204. Parental care may be subject to changes brought about by declarations which the parents – e.g. the unmarried father, §1626a I No. 1 BGB – may make themselves.[1] But changes will also follow by law where one of the parents who enjoy joint parental care dies or otherwise becomes unavailable, §1680 I, III; 1681, 1678 I BGB. Furthermore, Court orders may alter the situation in relation to parental care in a variety of cases, e.g. when the sole holder of parental care dies or becomes otherwise unavailable,[2] or where the child's welfare is endangered, §1666 BGB.

    1.   *See supra* No. 174sqq.
    2.   *See* §§1680 II, III; 1681, 1678 II BGB.

I. Suspension of Parental Care

205. The BGB knows several instances in which parental care may be suspended by Court order, i.e. where one or both of the parents formally retain their position as holders of parental care, but may not exercise this right any longer. This will happen where the Court declares a long-term inability to act as a parent, §1674 I BGB. This may be the case where a long-term prison sentence has been declared, but also if the parent is without (§1673 I BGB) or of limited legal capacity (§1673 II BGB). In the latter case the parent may still exercise parental care in certain areas, *see* §1673 II 2 BGB.

206. If joint parental care has been suspended, the other parent may act alone provided he holds parental care himself. Where this is not the case the Court will transfer parental care to the other parent provided this agrees with the child's welfare.

II. The End of Parental Care

207. According to its purpose, parental care regularly ends with the child's coming of age. This does not mean that all responsibility for the child ends.[1]

  1. *Cf.* e.g. the continuing duty to maintain, §§1603 II 2, 1609 BGB.

208. Parental care further ends with the death of the respective parent or where it is withdrawn by Court order, e.g. under §1666 BGB. Where the other parent does not hold parental care yet, the Court will then allocate parental care to this parent if this is not contrary to the child's welfare, §1680 II 1 BGB. Special rules apply to the unmarried father not yet vested with parental care: he will be granted parental care where this appears beneficial to the child's welfare, §1680 II 2 BGB. Where no other parent may fill the role as holder of parental care, the Court will appoint a guardian for the child, §1773 I BGB.

§14. PARENTAL CARE UPON SEPARATION/DIVORCE

I. Joint Parental Care

209. The reform law's guiding principle is that the parent's separation or divorce will not necessarily lead to a change in their (legal) relationship towards the child. When granting a divorce, the Court will only look into the position of children where one or both of the parents apply for sole parental care – and even then the Court is free to refuse the application.[1] Joint parental care may thus continue unaltered even through changes in the parents' marital status.

  1. *See* §§623 II 1 No. 1, 621 II 1 ZPO; 1671 I BGB.

210. The law does recognize the changes, though, which the parents' separation will bring about in the child's daily life. Where the parents cannot decide where the child is to live after their separation the Court may grant one of the parents the right to decide alone on this issue, §1628 BGB. Likewise, parents who continue to exercise parental care jointly can apply to the Court in a number of further questions, e.g. relating to contact (§1684 III), maintenance, or the child's upbringing (§1628 BGB).

211. §1687 BGB spells out a general division of competencies between the separated/divorced parents: As far as the child's routine daily life is concerned, the resident parent has the sole right to decide and to legally represent the child thus far (§1687 I 3 BGB). The non-resident parent enjoys a similar right during the time of the child's stay with him as far as the actual care taking is concerned.
The Family Law Court may restrict these rights should this be required in the interest of the child, §1687 II BGB. Issues of general importance, on the other hand, have to be decided by both parents jointly. Where danger is imminent, though, both parents may act alone, §1687 I BGB. How exactly the line between a

matter of daily routine and a matter of general importance is to be drawn is a question of considerable difficulty.

II. Sole Parental Care

212. A parent wishing to exercise parental care alone may apply to the Family Law Court for a corresponding order to be made in his favour. This will be granted if the other parent agrees (§1671 II No. 1 BGB) or if the Court is convinced that this would be in the best interest of the child (§1671 II No. 2 BGB).

Where both parents agree on the termination of their joint parental care the Court may not question their parental autonomy. This is only different should the child's welfare be endangered, §1697a BGB, or where the child himself has reached the age of fourteen and objects.

If the other parent opposes the application for sole parental care the Family Law Court may only grant the opposed order if it is convinced that sole parental care – in general and also as exercised by the applying parent in particular – is in the best interest of the child. This may be the case e.g. where severe discord prevails between the parents or where there is a history of abuse etc. In arriving at this decision the Court will also look at the child's wishes. It will take into consideration the child's best possible further development as well as the continuity in its upbringing.

213. Even if granting the order, the Court may retain certain areas for joint decisions and thus only partly comply with the request for sole parental care. The Code does not specify how parental care should be divided, thus leaving considerable discretion to the Courts to tailor individual orders. Any changes to parental care thus determined by Court order can only be effected by a new court order, even in the case of the parents' reconciliation, §1696 BGB.

214. Under certain circumstances, a collision between the procedures according to §1671 BGB (order on parental application) and according to §1666 BGB (order on official intervention because of risk to the child's welfare)[1] may occur. In this case, §1666 BGB and the state's duty to protect the child's welfare prevails.

    1.   *Supra* No. 200*sq.*

III. Sole Parental Care of the Unmarried Father

215. The new law generally tries to use the same legal framework for children irrespective of their parents' marital status. Still, some special rules apply to children whose parents were never married: e.g. where the non-resident father applies for sole parental care, the Court will grant this only where it is deemed to be beneficial to the child's wishes and where the mother does not oppose the order, §1672 I BGB.

§15. PROCEDURE

216. The procedure for parental care orders follows the rules for matters of non-contentious jurisdiction (FGG). The competent Court is the Family Law Court.[1] It will proceed according to the principle of judicial investigation, §12 FGG. The child and his parents have to be heard, §50a, b FGG. Special rules apply to protect the child from undesirable effects of the proceedings as best as possible, §52 FGG, and to ensure that his position is adequately represented.[2]

1. §23 I 2 No. 2 GVG.
2. E.g. the appointment of a procedural representive for the child, 'Verfahrenspfleger', §50 I FGG.

§16. CONTACT AND INFORMATION

I. Contact Between the Child and his Parents

217. §1626 BGB emphasizes that generally the child's welfare requires contact with both his parents. The Code accordingly grants the child a right to contact with his mother and father (§1684 I Hs 2 BGB). The corresponding parental right and duty to contact with the child is constitutionally protected in Art. 6 GG.[1]

Contact is realized through different means, often limited in time (weekend-visits, holidays, day-visits, via telephone, letters, etc.). Its extent and quality is mainly determined by agreement among the parents. As the child holds an own right to contact with his parents, his wishes shall be taken into account as far as possible.

1. BVerfGE 64, 180, 188.

218. The rights and duties to contact exist irrespective of who actually holds parental care. Contact may become an issue:

- where sole parental care is exercised by one parent. Here, the other parent is restricted to contact, which also is a right of the child,
- where joint parental care continues between the parents, but the child lives with only one of them. Here, the non-resident parent holds the right and duty to contact in addition to his continuing duties of parental responsibility,
- where the child lives in foster-care and both parents thus have a right and duty to contact,
- where the parents have been deprived of parental care. Even here a right to contact remains as far as this does not jeopardize the child's welfare.

219. §1684 III 1 BGB grants the Family Law Court the right to rule on the extent of contact and to regulate, limit or exclude such contact. A regulation may also include third persons (e.g. the new spouse of a parent) or impose conditions, e.g. the compulsory presence of a third person while the contact takes place. A complete exclusion or a limitation over a lengthy amount of time will only be permissible if this seems necessary to prevent considerable harm to the child's welfare. Court orders concerning contact are generally enforceable under the rules of non-contentious jurisdiction,[1] though no force may be applied against the child to ensure contact.[2]

Most often, a Court order will be applied for by one of the parents. It is possible, though, that the child himself takes the initiative as holder of an own right to contact. His application may be directed against the parent who prevents the contact as well as against the parent who refrains from exercising it. Where necessary, a curator ('Pfleger') may be appointed to act for the child before the court.

    1. §33 FGG.
    2. §33 II 2 FGG.

II. Contact with Other Persons

220. Since the *Child Law Reform Act 1998* additional persons have been invested with a legal right to contact with the child. Those now include the child's grandparents and his siblings (§1685 I BGB), the (former) spouse of a parent with whom the child has been living in the same household for a longer period of time, i.e. a step-parent, and other persons who acted as foster carers[1] for the child over some length of time (§1685 II BGB).

All such contact must be in the best interest of the child, who here does not have an own right of contact. Though it is generally up to the parents to determine this best interest, §1626 III 2 BGB points out especially that the child's welfare is served by contact with such persons as he has established special ties with.

    1. 'Familienpflege'.

III. Information

221. Effective exercise of parental care depends on sufficient information on the child's welfare, especially where the daily care is administered by one parent only. Irrespective of who actually holds parental care or exercises it §1686 BGB therefore grants both parents the right to demand information from each other about the personal condition of the child, in so far as this is compatible with the welfare of the child. The competent Court in case of dispute among the parents is the Family Law Court.

Chapter 7. Guardianship, Curatorship and Care and Control

§1. Introduction

222. – Guardianship ('Vormundschaft') is a long-standing institution under German law. Traditionally, guardianship means the all-encompassing care for another person regulated by law. Since the *Care and Control Act*[1] guardianship no longer applies to persons who have come of age but only in relation to minors.

– Curatorship ('Pflegschaft') means care for another person in a limited area only. It resembles guardianship the rules of which are largely applicable (§1915 BGB) but it may be used with both minors and majors.

– Care and Control ('Betreuung') is a new concept introduced by the *Care and Control Act* and only applies to majors. Here, a protector ('Betreuer') is appointed to care for persons who for reasons of physical, mental or psychological impediments can – either wholly or partially – no longer care for themselves.

1. 'Betreuungsgesetz' (BtG) of 12 December 1990.

223. Guardianship, Curatorship and Care and Control are all concerned with both private and public law issues. Today, the state regards it as her task to provide protection for persons unable to care for themselves. The actual care on the other hand is provided by individuals appointed to do so. The relation between carer and cared-for thus falls under the rules of private law, even though strong public-law elements remain, e.g. in the control exercized by the courts. Jurisdiction lies not with the Family Law Court, but with the Guardianship Courts which operate under the rules for non-contentious matters.

§2. Guardianship ('Vormundschaft')

I. Establishment

224. As a rule, guardianship is established by way of Court order made *ex officio* (§1774 S.1 BGB). Only as an exception will guardianship come about by law, i.e. upon the birth of an illegitimate child who requires a guardian (§1791c BGB) or where a child is freed for adoption under §1751 I 2 BGB.

225. According to §1773 BGB, a minor will be given a guardian:

– if he is not under parental authority (e.g. where the father has died and the mother has been deprived of parental authority);

– if his parents are not entitled to represent him in matters concerning either the person or the property (§1773 I BGB, e.g. where the father has died and the mother is still a minor);
– if his family situation cannot be ascertained, §1773 II BGB, e.g. in the case of a foundling.

A guardian may already be appointed before the child's birth. Where the appointment of a guardian becomes necessary under §1666 BGB[1] the jurisdiction lies with the Family Law Courts.

1. *See infra* No. 200*sqq.*

II. Choosing the Guardian

226. Where guardianship is established by Court order the Court is responsible for choosing the guardian or several guardians.[1] Where appropriate, the Court may also additionally appoint a supervising guardian (§1792 BGB).

1. Only under special circumstance, *cf.* §1797 BGB.

227. The main problem lies with finding a suitable person to act as guardian. The Code presumes that guardianship will usually be exercised by relatives or friends of the family who will act gratuitously. Today, reality often differs from this assumption. Where no suitable individual person is available to act as a guardian, the Court may therefore appoint the Youth Welfare Office or a society specially endorsed for this purpose instead (§§1791a, b BGB).

The law provides guidelines to be followed by the Court in the act of nomination: Firstly, the persons nominated by the child's parents are qualified, if the parents at the time of their death were entitled to personal and financial care of the child, §§1776, 1777 BGB. Where no such person has been nominated, the Court will select a suitable guardian according to his personal and financial position, the parent's presumed wishes, relations of consanguinity and affinity and to any personal ties the ward has formed as well as to the ward's religious confession, §1779 II BGB.

228. A person who is incompetent to enter into legal transactions may not be appointed as guardian, §1780 BGB; minors or persons under care and control as well as such persons excluded by the parents are generally deemed unsuitable by the law, §1781 BGB.

229. Every German is under an obligation to accept the role as guardian proposed to him except where special reasons listed in §1786 BGB apply. Should a person nevertheless refuse he may be compelled by fines and be liable for any damages caused to the ward, §§1787, 1788 BGB.

The chosen guardian is then appointed by the Guardianship Court and placed under the obligation to conduct the guardianship faithfully and conscientiously. The obligation is performed by clasp of hand, §1789 BGB.

III. Personal Care

230. Guardianship fills the place of parental authority. The guardian therefore enjoys the full right and duty for the ward's personal and financial care, including the right to legally represent the ward, §1793 BGB. The rules relating to personal care exercised by parents apply, e.g. the duty to consider the growing maturity of the ward.[1]

1. §§1800, 1631–1633 and 1793, 1626 II BGB.

231. The Guardianship Court exercises supervision over the entire activity of the guardian(s), it is assisted herein by the Youth Welfare Office. The Court is given the power to intervene against violation of the guardian's duties by way of appropriate orders and prohibitions, including the attribution of penalties, §1837 II BGB. Where the carrying on of the office would jeopardize the ward's interests, especially because of a breach of duty by the guardian, the Court may also discharge the guardian, §1886 BGB. Special rules apply in relation to the child's religious upbringing.[1]

1. *Cf.* §§1801 I, 1909 I BGB.

IV. Legal Representation

232. As far as legal representation of the ward is concerned, the guardian is subject to stricter rules than those applicable under parental authority: The area of dispositions in respect of which the Guardianship Court's approval is required exceeds that under parental care.[1] Just in the same way as a parent the guardian is prevented from legal representation under §§181 and 1795 BGB.

1. Compare §1821–23 and §§1643, 1645 BGB.

V. Financial Care

233. In managing the ward's financial affairs the guardian just as the parents shall aim at the conservation, augmentation and possible use of the child's assets. To ensure this the guardian has to provide an inventory. He is subsequently placed under considerable and specific restrictions in relation e.g. to the investment of money, the deposit of bearer securities or the disposal of claims.[1] The guardian is not permitted to use the ward's property for himself nor may he make gifts as the ward's representative except out of a moral duty or common decency, §§1805f BGB.

1. *Cf.* §§1802*sq.* BGB.

234. The Guardianship Court with assistance from the Youth Welfare Office will supervise the financial care.[1] To this end, the guardian is requested by law to provide information and to report to the Court at least once a year, §§1840–43 BGB. Again, the Court may act appropriately if the guardian violates his duties.[2]

1. As regulated in §1837 II BGB, §53 III 5 SGB VIII.
2. *See supra* and §§1837, 1886 BGB.

VI. The Relationship between Guardian and Ward

235. The relationship between guardian and ward contains strong elements of the mandate (§§662ff BGB). Where the guardian incurs expenses he is thus under the provisions of §§669, 670 BGB entitled to an advance payment or reimbursement from the ward. If the ward is without means, the state treasury will provide these payments instead, §1836 I, IV BGB. Services provided by the guardian are generally not recoverable except where they pertain to his trade or profession.

According to the concept of the Code, guardianship shall generally be conducted gratuitously, §1836 I 1 BGB. As an exception from this rule the Code allows for appropriate compensation in the case of acknowledged professional guardianship, §1836 I 2, III BGB.

VII. Ending Guardianship

236. The guardianship comes to an end upon the lapse of the conditions that originally led to its constitution, §§1882, 1773 BGB, e.g. where the ward reaches majority. Likewise, it ends with the ward's death.[1] It should be noted that the end of guardianship is separate from the term of office of a specific guardian. As it relates to the capacity of the ward it will continue through a change of guardian. The guardian may also be discharged by the Court if the ward's best interests are jeopardized by his remaining in office, §1886 BGB.

1. *Cf.* §1884 BGB for details.

237. Upon termination of his office – for whatever reason – the guardian shall deliver the administered property to the ward and render account of his administration to the ward and the Guardianship Court, §§1890*sqq.* BGB.

§3. CURATORSHIP ('PFLEGSCHAFT')

I. General

238. Curatorship constitutes a special legal framework relating to the care for a person or a financial entity.[1] Grounds for an order establishing curatorship can be found throughout the civil and public law. Here, we will only look at those forms of curatorship closely connected with family law:

1. E.g. an estate, §1961 BGB.

239. Structurally, curatorship over a person resembles guardianship. The main difference is that the curator's range of responsibilities is not all-encompassing, but closely limited. Still, the provisions governing guardianship are applicable *mutatis mutandis*, unless the law provides otherwise. Such differing provisions are to be found e.g. as:

– no supervising curator will be appointed, §1915 II BGB;
– rules as to qualification for a guardian do not apply (§§1916, 1917 BGB);
– the termination of curatorship is concerned (§1918ff BGB).

240. Curatorship is established by way of law or by order of the Guardianship Court or – less often – the Family Law Court. The Guardianship Court will be responsible for the appointment and the supervision of the curator.

II. Forms of Curatorship

241. The law knows different forms of curatorship. Of special importance to the family lawyer is supplementary curatorship as described in §1909 BGB. In addition to the continuing parental care, supplementary curatorship is given where and to the extent that parents are unable to attend to matters relating to the child. Appointment does not follow the rules for guardianship (§1916), the Court may therefore make an appointment without being bound by parental suggestions.

A curator can also be appointed for the unborn child (§1912 BGB) where such support seems necessary for the protection of its future rights. Lastly, curatorship can be arranged where the conditions for a guardianship order exist, but no guardian has yet been appointed. Here, curatorship will fill the gap created (§1909 III BGB).

§4. CARE AND CONTROL ('BETREUUNG')

242. The *Care and Control Act*[1] abolished several legal institutions hitherto existent: declaration of incompetence, guardianship over persons who have reached majority and curatorship over persons suffering from physical infirmity. In place of these, the Act introduced the concept of 'Care and Control' ('Betreuung'). Jurisdiction remains with the Guardianship Courts.

   1.   Betreuungsgesetz (BtG) of 12 December 1990, in force since 1 January 1992.

I. Appointment of a Protector

243. The Code describes the grounds on which a protector is to be appointed in rather general terms: An appointment will thereafter be made if a person of full age is at least partly unable to take care of his affairs by reason of physical ailment or physical, mental or psychological impediment.

244. The appointment shall only be made where and in so far as it is required. This 'requirement principle' is then further developed: Care and Control is not necessary where affairs can be taken care of just as efficiently by a person with powers of attorney or other assistants. The law thus leaves room for private law solutions to the problems arising.

The requirement principle furthermore asks that Care and Control be restricted to such areas in which the person concerned is indeed in need of assistance. Only in special cases will a protector thus be invested with all-encompassing powers of representation, usually they will be specified and restricted to e.g. health matters, management of financial assets, etc.

245. There is also a limitation in time: when making the order, the court has to set a date for possible 'revision' of the order, this must lie within the five years following the issuing of the order.[1]

    1. *See* §69 I No. 5 69c I FGG.

II. Forms of Protectorship

246. Finding suitable protectors can be difficult. This explains the considerable variety of options on who to appoint that the law allows for. The starting point is the private natural person who will – ideally – act *pro bono*. As such a person will often not be available, Care and Control may also be exercised for remuneration and by associations or authorities. Even then, though, the new law strives to retain some personal element: where possible, not the association/authority will be appointed as protector, but an individual member within this institution (§1897 II 1, 2 BGB).

Appointments will be made according to suitability and capability to represent the protégé adequately. Priority is given to any nomination made by the person under care if following this would not be contrary to his welfare. Likewise, his refusal to accept a certain protector will also be taken into consideration as well as aspects of kinship, familial ties and possible conflicting interests (§1897 IV, V BGB).

III. The Protector's Rights and Duties

247. In carrying out his duties, the paramount consideration for the protector shall be the welfare of the person under his care. The new law places special emphasis on preserving a maximum degree of self-determination for the person placed under Care and Control. The protector shall thus consult with the protégé and where possible comply with his wishes (§1901 II, III BGB).

248. To enable the protector to efficiently carry out his duties, he is invested with the right to represent the person under his care in judicial and extrajudicial matters (§1902 BGB); this may be accompanied by further rights, e.g. to determine contact, residence, etc.

This right to legal representation is curtailed by the law in multiple ways: First, most restrictions used in the law of guardianship apply via §1908i I 1 BGB.

Secondly, the special provisions of Care and Control contain numerous further restrictions. Thirdly, it is important to note that even where the protector enjoys the right of representation and decisions making, the person under his care still retains full power to enter into legal transactions by himself, unless he is *in concreto* legally incompetent in the sense of the general rules found in §104 No. 2 BGB.

This overlap of responsibilities may cause problems in the case where both protector and protégé act on the same matter but in diverging ways. The rule is then that the act prior in time will be valid, but where the acts are valid independently of each other both will remain valid.

249. The law recognizes, nevertheless, that there are limits to the principle of self-determination and that in the best interest of the person under care this may have to be checked. Where this is necessary to prevent substantial jeopardy the court may therefore order that any declaration made by the person under care needs the protector's consent.

IV. Termination

250. A protector may be discharged by the Guardianship Court for various reasons, e.g. if his qualification is no longer assured, or if the person under his care suggests someone equally qualified (§1908b I, III BGB). Such discharge does not pertain to the placement under Care and Control, but it will only terminate the individual protector's office. A new protector will then have to be appointed speedily.

251. Care and Control as a whole may be cancelled only if the conditions therefor cease to exist (§1908d BGB), e.g. if the protégé no longer suffers from the relevant ailment. Such cancellation may be applied for by the protégé himself. Should Care and Control initially have been ordered on his own application such wish for cancellation has to be obeyed by the Courts unless the care should now be required *ex officio* (§1908d II BGB).

Chapter 8. Financial Support Among Relatives

§1. GENERAL

252. The right to be maintained by another person may be based on statute or on contract. Under German law, statutory rights to maintenance can arise between (divorced) spouses, relatives in direct line and between the unmarried parents of a common child. Maintenance claims are recoverable by law. An action may also be directed to future regular claims[1] or prior to the actual claim asking for information to be furnished in respect of the obligee's financial capacity. The jurisdiction lies with the Family Law Court.[2]

    1.   §258 ZPO.
    2.   §§23 I 2 No. 6, 7 GVG.

253. Next to civil-law maintenance claims we find the system of social security, also directed towards provision in case of need. Difficult problems may arise from this juxtaposition, as generally maintenance can only be claimed in the absence of other sources of provision. Important for solving this conflict is §2 I BSHG where it is set out that social security benefits are subsidiary to maintenance claims under civil law and that the state may reclaim any payments made from the obligee.[1]

    1.   *Cf. also* §91 BSHG.

§2. FINANCIAL SUPPORT AMONG RELATIVES

254. According to §1601 BGB only relatives in direct line are obliged to furnish maintenance to each other, e.g. parents towards their children, grandparents towards the parents and their offspring and *vice versa*. Siblings are not obliged to maintain each other under German law. The maintenance duties of parents in relation to their minor children as a special form of maintenance among relatives of direct line follow special rules set out in the next chapter.

Generally, a claim for maintenance may be made under two conditions: the claimant's lack of means and the obligee's financial capacity.

I. Lack of Means

255. Only a person who is unable to support himself is entitled to maintenance, §1602 I BGB. This means that the claimant does not have a sufficient income from either gainful employment or his property or the equitable conversion of his assets. Employment may be deemed suitable even if it lies outside the scope of the claimant's education or standard of living. Even the care for a child does not *per se* free the claimant from the obligation to pursue at least part-time employment where this seems equitable.

II. Financial Capacity

256. A person is deemed to be of sufficient financial capacity where – taking into account his other obligations – he is able to provide for maintenance without jeopardizing the appropriate maintenance for himself, §1603 I BGB. The Courts will not only regard the obligee's actual income, but consider what income he could reasonably achieve ('fictional income'). Income from property will be taken into account, though there is no obligation to actually convert assets.[1] Both lack of means and financial capacity may be only partially resulting in a reduced claim/obligation.

1. BGH FamRZ 1986, 48.

III. Maintenance Claim

257. The maintenance includes the entire necessities of life, including expenses for appropriate training or – where needed – education (§1610 II BGB). It does not include provision for maintenance that the claimant himself would be under an obligation to pay nor the cost of old age provision.

The degree of maintenance to be paid is measured by the claimant's standard of living and is thus not automatically limited to the bare necessities. On the other hand, it will to some extent also depend on the obligee's standard of living as this is taken into account when determining his financial capacity (§1603 I BGB).

258. The maintenance shall be provided by the disbursement of a periodic payment, to be made monthly in advance, §1612 I 1, III BGB. If special reasons justify this, the obligee may on request be allowed to provide the maintenance in kind. On top of the monthly payments, the claimant may demand further financial assistance in the case of exceptional and unusually expensive necessities, §1613 II BGB.

259. The relationship that gives rise to the maintenance claim as such is not subject to prescription (§194 II BGB), but each individual claim made will prescribe in four years (§197 BGB). Importantly, maintenance for the past may only be demanded in special circumstances to protect the debtor, who might not be aware of his duty, from high and unexpected maintenance arrears. Retrospective performance may thus only be demanded if the debtor had already been requested to furnish information in respect of the claim, when he was given notice of default or when the claim for maintenance became pending in Court.

260. An exemption from these limitations is made under §1613 II BGB if the obligee seems not worthy of such protection, i.e. if the claimant was prevented for legal or specific factual reasons from raising the claim. The debtor then is protected by a hardship clause in §1613 III BGB: no or at least not the full claim can be made if this would impose undue hardship on the obligee. Claims made for unusually exceptional necessities under §1613 II are fully claimable for the past, §1613 II No.1 BGB.

IV. Restrictions

261. The duty to maintain is restricted or even removed entirely where mainte-nance payments would seem inequitable in the light of serious offences on the part of the claimant. According to §1611 BGB this may be the case where the person entitled to maintenance:

– became needy by his own moral delinquency,
– grossly neglected his duty to maintain himself to the detriment of the obligee,
– was guilty of an intentional serious breach of duty due to the person obliged or his close relative.

262. The maintenance claim becomes extinguished on the death of either the claimant or the obligee. Only in so far as retrospective payments or damages for such payments are concerned or prospective claims were already due may claims still be made even after the death of one of the parties. Also, where the claimant's heirs are unable to cover the burial expenses, they have to be paid by the obligee (§1615 II BGB).

263. The statutory duty to maintain can be modified by contract, but only within the limits set by §1614 BGB: most importantly, this means that future maintenance claims may not be waived.

V. Rank

264. Difficult questions of rank may arise if the person in need can raise claims against several different obligees: Here the claimant's spouse is liable before his relatives (§1608 BGB). The relatives will still be liable to the extent that the spouse – due to his limited financial capacity – is unable to cover the cost.

Among relatives, the claimant's descendants are liable before the relatives in ascending line (§1606 BGB). Within each group, those closer in line are liable before the more remote (§1606 II BGB). Several equally close relatives are liable proportionally to their earnings and property circumstances (§1606 III 1 BGB). Where a relative is exempted from the duty to maintain because of lack of sufficient funds, the relative next to him in line will become liable instead, §1607 I BGB.

265. Similar problems arise where a person is obliged in relation to several needy claimants, but is unable to provide maintenance for all of them. According to §1609 BGB, here any minor unmarried children precede the other children, the other children (i.e. those married or of age) will precede the other descendants, who will again precede relatives in the ascending line.

VI. Recourse

266. It is possible that a relative or parent paid maintenance even though he was not – or only subsidiarily – liable to such payments. He then can seek repayment of such expenses from the recipient under the general rules of restitution according to §812I 2 BGB.[1] The payee may prefer to take recourse to the person actually liable. Here, the Code provides for a *cessio legis* to facilitate the realization of such claims:

– where a relative only had to pay maintenance because the prosecution within the country of legal action against the relative originally liable is not possible or considerably difficult (§1607 II BGB), the claim against the latter passes to the payee;[2]
– where a third person maintains a child believing he is the child's father and §1607 II applies, he will then by law be able to seek repayment from the child's natural father. A hindrance to the prosecution in the sense of §1607 II BGB will already be accepted where the child's paternity hasn't been challenged and the child thus does not (yet) have a claim against his natural father. Here, maintenance may even be claimed for the past.[3]

> 1. But *cf.* §814 BGB for limitations.
> 2. *Cf.* §§1607 II, III, 1608 BGB for a similar *cessio legis* in relation to spouses or parents.
> 3. *See* §1613 II No. 2a BGB.

§3. THE PARENTS' DUTY TO MAINTAIN THEIR CHILDREN

I. General

267. Special provisions apply to one particular maintenance duty among relatives, that is to the parents' duty to provide for their children. In relation to minors the duty to maintain follows from the principle of parental care. This interdependence of parental care and the duty to maintain is reflected in the fact that – unlike any other obligees – a parent may fulfil his obligation to contribute to the maintenance of the minor unmarried child by providing care and upbringing (§1606 III 2 BGB).[1]

> 1. *See infra* No. 275*sq.*

268. The situation is different where children who have come of age are concerned. As a rule, it is assumed that they are self-reliant. But even here the parental relationship may lead to a continuing duty to maintain where the child has in fact not yet reached economic independence, e.g. because of his continuing education. Following a long tradition, the statute treats the married child as one who has reached majority. This is based on the assumption that upon marriage the child reaches economic independence. Under a changed perception of marriage today this is often not the case and consequently may lead to unjust results.

269. The following chapter deals with the special statutory provisions relating to maintenance claims of children against their parents. Where those do not apply, the maintenance duties will follow the general rules for maintenance between relatives set out *supra.*[1]

> 1. *Supra* No. 254*sqq.*

II. The Child's Lack of Means

270. In contrast to other claimants, the minor unmarried child is not requested to realize assets to provide for his maintenance, *cf.* §1602 II BGB. Also, the minor is under no obligation to seek gainful employment as education and training take precedence. This is true even for a child who has come of age but still follows an education unless it would seem inequitable in the light of the parent's precarious financial situation and the ready availability of education-related work for the child.

III. The Parent's Financial Capacity

271. Different from other obligees, parents may not claim reduced financial capacity on the grounds of having to uphold their standard of living. They have to apply all means at their disposal to their own and their children's maintenance in an equal measure, §1603 II 1 BGB. This obligation exists not only in relation to the parents' minor children, but since the *Child Support Act 1998* also in relation to any unmarried children up to the age of twenty-one while those are living in their parents house and still undergo general schooling, §1603 II 2 BGB.

Even under strained financial circumstances the parents are thus committed to solidarity with their children; this applies equally to major children who still follow an education. Parents can thus claim financial incapacity only if there is another relative obliged to provide maintenance or if the child's maintenance can be provided for from the principal of his property, §1603 III 3 BGB.

272. §1603 II BGB asks parents even to realize assets. In the light of these demands the Courts have developed a system (laid down in Tables) to prevent the parents falling under social security as a result of this extensive duty to maintain. The parent will thus even in relation to a child always be entitled to the 'necessary retention' (e.g. 1999: 1500,- DM/month for an employed person in relation to a minor; 1800,-DM in relation to a child of age).[1]

1.   Düsseldorfer Tabelle, FamRZ 1999, 766.

IV. The Maintenance Claim

A. Degree of Maintenance

273. The degree of maintenance is determined according to the general rule of §1610 BGB. Again, the Courts use Tables relating to the parent's income and the child's age to ensure relative uniformity of judicial decisions. The Code does not proclaim a minimal sum, but provides for statutory standard rates and the possibility to seek a suitable percentage of those rates in a special simplified procedure.[1]

The cost of education or training is of special importance to the maintenance of children. Parents are under an obligation to provide education for a suitable length of time, even after the child has reached majority. Individual circumstances have to

be taken into account to determine the extent of this obligation and extensive judicature exists on this point. The child, on the other hand, is under an obligation to
follow his studies purposefully and he may lose his claim if this does not appear to
be the case without sufficient reason.[2]

1. *Cf.* §1612a–c BGB and §§645*sqq.* ZPO and the 'RegelbetragsVO'.
2. BGH FamRZ 1998, 671; 1987, 470.

274. The Courts are rather restrictive in the amount of maintenance they award
to children who have come of age. Even where the parent's standard of living is
very high they will usually grant amounts only slightly above public education
grants.[1]

1. Düsseldorfer Tabelle: ca 1.100,-DM/month, *see* FamRZ 1999, 766.

B. Mode of Provision

275. Maintenance for minor unmarried children can be fulfilled by providing
care and upbringing, §1606 III 2 BGB. Furthermore, if parents have to provide
maintenance for an unmarried child, they are not under an obligation to fulfil the
claim by monthly payments, but it is up to them to determine in which manner and
for what future period in advance the maintenance will be provided. Most importantly, this includes provision of maintenance in kind, e.g. by offering board and
lodging, clothing, etc. With minors, this fulfilment in kind is the rule, but parents
may also choose it in relation to their children who have come of age. On petition
of the child, the Family Law Court may alter the parents' decision if special
grounds apply, §1612 II 2 BGB. The petition can be raised by the minor himself.

276. The restriction or removal of the duty to maintain as spelled out in §1611
BGB does not apply to maintenance provided by parents towards their minor
unmarried children (§1611 II BGB). In exceptional cases – e.g. where the child has
attempted to kill a parent – the claim may be forfeited according to the general
rules of equity, §242 BGB.

V. Procedure

277. Statutory maintenance claims can be pursued before the ordinary Civil
Courts. Jurisdiction lies with the Family Law Court.[1] Some special procedural rules
apply, though,[2] in order to invest the Court with sufficient inquisitorial powers to
ensure that the decision is placed on a reliable basis. For maintenance claims of
minor children against a parent who does not live with the child a simplified procedure exists to grant speedy and effective realization of the child's rights.

1. §§23b I 2 No. 5, 6 GVG.
2. *Cf.* §§642 *sq.* ZPO.

§4. Special Provisions for Unmarried Parents

278. Since the reform of Child Law in 1998[1] the provisions relating to maintenance apply to all children alike, whether their parents are married or not. Few spe-
cialities remain in relation to children of unmarried parents:

1. Child Law Reform Act (Kindschaftsrechtsreformgesetz) of 16 February 1997 and Child
   Support Act (Kindesunterhaltsgesetz) of 6 April 1998.

279. Upon the petition of the child, the Court may provide an interim order to
the effect that the man who has acknowledged paternity or who is presumed to be
the child's natural father shall pay maintenance to the child for the first three
months after the child's birth. The petition may be presented even before the child's
birth to ensure financial security immediately after confinement.

280. Secondly, the Code grants a limited maintenance claim to the child's
mother to be made against the father, §1615l BGB. Both the Courts and legislation
have systematically increased the scope of this claim over the years:

– Without having to fulfil further criteria, the mother can claim maintenance for the
  period of six weeks prior to, and eight weeks after the child's birth, as well as the
  cost arising from the birth or pregnancy, even if they occurred outside this time.
– Further maintenance can only be claimed if the mother is unable – or only partially able – to pursue gainful employment as a consequence of an illness relating to the pregnancy or birth, or because the child can not otherwise be cared
  for. To determine this question the Courts apply the same rules as in the case of
  a divorced spouse seeking maintenance under §1570 BGB.[1]

1. *See supra* No. 105*sqq.*

281. This claim is also limited in time: the father's duty to maintenance begins
not earlier then four months before the confinement. It ends not later than three
years after the child's birth except where this would seem grossly inequitable considering the welfare of the child. It may then continue as long as the child requires
care and the reasons establishing gross inequity apply.
The Courts definition of such 'gross inequity' plays a central role. It should be
kept in mind that the claim exists mainly for the sake of the child's welfare; in spite
of the wording the provision should thus not be used too restrictively.

282. The general rules for maintenance as between relatives apply (§§1615l III 1
BGB); the claim therefore depends on the mother's lack of own means and the
father's financial capacity. The degree of maintenance follows the mother's standard of living. The claim may not be waived for the future.[1] For questions of rank
see §1615l III BGB.

1. §1614 BGB. This is different where a divorced spouse raises a claim, *see supra* No. 105*sqq.*

283. Where it is the unmarried father who actually cares for the child he will be
entitled to similar claims, §1615l V BGB.

Part III. Matrimonial Property Law

Introduction

284. The German Civil Code does not know a compulsory property regime during marriage. The spouses are – within certain limits – free to regulate questions of property in a binding marriage contract, §1408 I BGB. Likewise, they may thus exclude the equalization of support (pension splitting), §1408 II BGB.

In §§1408*sq.* BGB the Code sets out guidelines for such contractual property rights and presents two model contractual regimes, separation of property ('Gütertrennung') and community of property ('Gütergemeinschaft'). Where – as in the majority of cases – no such agreement is made, the statutory regime of community of accrued gains ('Zugewinngemeinschaft') will apply, as well as pension splitting. Both are regulated in the Code, §§1363*sq.* BGB.[1]

1. *Cf. infra* No. 296 *sqq.*

Chapter 1. The Contractual Matrimonial Property Regimes

§1. Separation of Property

285. Separation of property will occur where the spouses have formally agreed on such a regime or where they have agreed to forego the statutory property regime, §1414 BGB.

Under separation of property each spouse manages his property independently. No limitations to managing or disposal derive from the marital status. There will be pension splitting, though, unless otherwise agreed upon. Joint property may arise only according to general rules, e.g. should the spouses jointly enter into a transaction. Often one of the spouses transfers property or other assets to the other spouse in the course of the marriage. Should the marriage be dissolved afterwards, problems may arise if he then wishes to regain such assets, as the law does not provide special rules for this case. Recuperation may be tried under §531 II BGB as revocation of a gift.[1]

> 1. But *cf.* the problems arising from the Court's restrictive interpretation of donations among spouses ('ehebedingte Zuwendungen')

§2. Community of Property

286. Where the spouses have formally agreed on community of property the rules found in §§1415–82 BGB apply: All assets become joint property of the spouses (common property). Property which comes into ownership of husband or wife during the marriage – as long as the property regime is not changed – will also automatically and instantly belong to the common property. There is no need to transfer individual items by legal transaction, but upon entering the regime, common property comes into existence by universal succession, §1416 II BGB. Where necessary, the Land Register has to be amended accordingly, §1416 II BGB.

287. Certain exemptions are made from the rule of automatic common property. Each spouse still acts independently as the sole owner in the case of:

- Special property ('Sondergut'), §1417 BGB, which comprises items which cannot be transferred by legal transaction (e.g. usufruct).
- Separate property ('Vorbehaltsgut'), §1418 BGB. This comprises items (a) which have been declared by marriage contract as such or (b) which a spouse receives *mortis causa* or which are gratuitously transferred to him by a third party if specified as such or (c) which are received as a result of surrogation for an item belonging to separate property.

288. In relation to the common property, both partners enjoy the same rights and duties unless otherwise agreed upon. Considerable mutual restrictions apply:

According to §1419 I BGB no spouse may dispose of his part of the common property nor of individual items which belong to the common property. The common property is managed jointly by the spouses unless they agree otherwise in the marriage contract, §1421 BGB.

This means that the spouses are under a mutual obligation to cooperate (§1451 BGB) and as a rule may only act jointly where the disposal of or litigation relating to common property is concerned.[1] This obligation to act jointly leads to complications in legal transactions. Sole property management by one of the partners – which may be agreed upon by the spouses in the marriage contract – implies on the other hand considerable dependence for the non-managing spouse.[2]

    1. For exceptions *see* §§1450 II, 1454, 1455 BGB.
    2. *Cf.* 1422, 1423–32 BGB.

289. Creditors may demand satisfaction from the common property for obligations entered into by husband or wife, §1459 I, 1437 I BGB.[1] The spouses are furthermore personally liable with their special and separate property for their respective personal obligations. If they have agreed on joint management, the special and separate property will also be liable for personal obligations of the other spouse, §1459 II BGB.

    1. For exceptions from this rule *see* §1460–62, 1438–40 BGB.

290. Each spouse may institute proceedings for the dissolution of the community of property by act of Court, §1447*sq.* BGB. It further ends with the dissolution of the marriage unless otherwise agreed upon; *cf.* §1483*sq.* BGB for the continuation of community of property after the death of one of the spouses.

§3. Formalities

291. Where a couple thus agrees to regulate their property relations by marriage contract they have to observe certain formal requirements and limitations:

– The marriage contract must be concluded in the simultaneous presence of both parties and must be recorded by a notary, §1410 BGB.
– The matrimonial property regime may not be determined by reference to a law no longer in force or to a foreign one, §1409 BGB. Foreign legal provisions may nevertheless govern the marriage under the rules of conflict of laws where applicable.[1]
– After concluding the marriage, the spouses are free to cancel or alter the property regime in force before, §1408 I BGB.

    1. *Cf.* Art. 15 II EGBGB.

292. In addition to agreeing on or excluding one of the property regimes, the spouses may also alter single provisions within one of the regimes set out or simply opt out of pension splitting. Where the spouses have not agreed otherwise, the exclusion of pensions splitting – just as the mere opting out of the statutory property regime – will lead to the presumption that they opted for separation of property, §1414 S.2 BGB.

293. How far the spouses should furthermore be free to regulate their property relationships in ways different from the models set out in the code (i.e. community of accrued gains, separation of property or community of property) is a matter of dispute. There seems to be no justification, though, to restrict the spouses' freedom of contract further than the rules set out *supra* and the general rules of civil law demand.

§4. The Register of Marital Property

294. So that their property agreements may be enforceable against third parties, the spouses may apply for registration in the Register of Marital Property at the Local Court (Amtsgericht), §1558 BGB. Property regulations can be registered where they vary from the rule of statutory property regime and this divergence might affect the interests of third parties.

295. The Register enjoys negative reliance only,[1] meaning that where a regulation has not been registered it may not be invoked against a third party, e.g. a creditor, unless the relevant provisions of the marriage contract were actually known to that party. Apart from this, registration or non-registration is without influence as to the validity of the property arrangements among the spouses.

1.   So-called 'negative Publizität'.

Chapter 2. The Statutory Matrimonial Property Regime

296. If the spouses have not formally agreed otherwise, the statutory property regime of community of accrued gains applies. Here, during the marriage each spouse manages his property independently and only after the marriage is ended an equalization of accrued gains is achieved, §1363*sqq.* BGB.

Still, some restrictions apply during the marriage. The independent management is limited in several ways by the law to protect the other spouse's interests effectively: §§1365, 1369 and 1370 BGB.

§1. DISPOSAL OF PROPERTY IN ITS ENTIRETY, §1365 BGB

297. According to §1365 BGB, a spouse may enter into an obligation to dispose of his property in its entirety only with the consent of the other spouse. If he enters into such an obligation without the required consent he may fulfil such an obligation only if the other spouse gives his consent.

298. To define the term 'disposal of property in its entirety' accurately meets with considerable difficulties:

- The Courts have pointed out that the term is to be interpreted from an economic point of view. Therefore, even the disposal of *one* item of property alone may suffice to fulfil the requirements of §1365 BGB if this item constitutes the entire property of the spouse or at least nearly the entire property (less than 10–15 per cent remaining).
- What a spouse receives in return for the transaction is not to be taken into account.
- The acting spouse does not have to be aware of the fact that he is disposing of his property to such an extent. The Federal Court of Justice (BGH) has set out another important requirement, though, and has substantially curtailed the sort of transactions §1365 would apply to: The other party to the transaction has to know positively that the spouse's (near) entire property is involved in the transaction or this must have been evident on the ground of his knowledge of the couple's financial situation. Where the other party does not know that, §1365 BGB is seen not to apply and thus no consent is required.[1]

    1. BGHZ 43, 174.

299. Where the transaction falls within the scope of §1365 BGB, consent will be required for the obligation entered into as well as for the actual transferral of the property.

§2. Disposal of Household Items, §1369 BGB

300. §1369 BGB limits the spouses' power to dispose of household items. A spouse living under the statutory property regime may thus only dispose of items in the conjugal household belonging to himself – or may undertake an obligation to do so – if the other spouse consents thereto. It does not matter in this context whether the item in question is owned solely by the acting spouse or whether it is held jointly. Items serving only the personal use of one of the spouses are not covered by §1369 BGB.

§3. Consent

301. Where consent is thus required according to §1365 or §1369 BGB, the other spouse is free to consent to the transaction or not. Should he unreasonably refuse his consent, the Guardianship Court ('Vormundschaftsgericht') may, upon the application of one spouse, substitute the consent. The same will apply where the other spouse is by reason of sickness or absence prevented from making a declaration, §§1369 II, 1365 II BGB.

A unilateral transaction carried out without the requisite consent is ineffective, §1367 BGB. A contract concluded without that consent may in contrast be effective if the other spouse later ratifies it, §1366 BGB.

302. The other party to the contract is entitled to revoke the contract until its ratification. Revocation is excluded if he knew that the spouse was married unless the spouse untruthfully claimed to have been given the necessary consent. If the other party demands that the required ratification be produced the consenting spouse can only grant such ratification; any prior ratification will be ineffective. Such ratification has to be declared within two weeks from the receipt of the demand, otherwise it will be deemed to have been refused. Where the ratification is refused, the contract is ineffective.

303. To prevent the acting spouse from continuing with the (ineffective) transaction by refusing to reclaim the transferred property, §1368 BGB grants the other spouse the right to enforce in Court the rights arising out of the ineffectiveness of the disposition against the third party.

304. In the absence of the required consent, no *bona fide* purchase is possible as §§1365, 1369 BGB constitute an absolute restraint on alienation.[1]

1.   *Cf.* BGHZ 40, 218.

Chapter 3. Equalization of Accrued Gains

305. The statutory property regime may end in various ways. Upon the death of one of the spouses the ensuing equalization of accrued gains is realized by increasing the statutory share in the estate by one quarter (§§1371 I, 1931 BGB), irrelevant of whether the spouse actually made a gain in the individual case.[1]

1.   *See infra* No. 320 *sqq.*

306. Upon divorce, annulment, contractual opting-out or death without the surviving spouse being either heir or the recipient of a legacy an equalization claim is granted according to §§1371 *sqq.* BGB.

§1. THE ACCRUED GAINS

307. If the gains accrued by one spouse during the time of the marriage exceed those of the other spouse, the latter is entitled to one half of the difference in surplus as an equalization claim, §1378 I BGB.

308. Who of the spouses is entitled to this claim and to what it amounts is determined by comparing each of the spouses' assets at the beginning ('initial assets', §1374 BGB) and at the termination ('final assets', §1375 BGB) of the statutory property regime. Only in the case of divorce the relevant date for determining the final assets is set at the date when the application for divorce becomes pendant, §1384 BGB. 'Accrued gains' thus means the amount by which the final assets of a spouse exceed his initial assets, §1373 BGB.

309. In litigation, it may be difficult for a spouse to know what his partner's initial and final assets actually amount to. §1377 BGB presumes for that purpose that where the spouses jointly established the contents and value of their respective initial assets in an inventory, this inventory is accurate. Each spouse may demand co-operation in the drawing up of this inventory.

Where no such inventory was drawn up – as in the majority of cases – §1377 BGB further presumes the final assets of a spouse to represent his accrued gains, i.e. that no initial assets existed. Each spouse is therefore obliged to proof the existence and amount of initial assets if he wants to claim to have had such.

310. To make their final assets transparent, each spouse according to §1379 BGB is obliged to furnish information on the contents of his final assets to the other spouse. In the case of annulment or divorce, such a claim may already be made following the petitioning for the dissolution, §1379 II BGB.

§2. ADJUSTMENTS

311. The Code allows for several adjustments to the actual amount of initial and final assets in the interest of a true equalization of accrued gains.

312. In the eyes of the law, assets which have been acquired by a spouse after the beginning of the statutory property regime as a result of death, in consideration of a prospective right to inheritance, or through a gift or a furnishing, are made independent of the conjugal community and bear no connection with the joint accruement through the marriage. According to §1374 II BGB, they are therefore to be treated as if they had been made *before* the beginning of the statutory property regime and are – after deduction of obligations – to be included in the *initial* assets.

313. A similar method is used to equalize any undue diminishing of a spouse's final assets (which he may be interested in so to lower his surplus and improve his position in relation to the other spouse). Gratuitous dispositions which a spouse made and by which he did not comply with a moral obligation or one which arose from principles of common decency, assets that were wasted, or transactions implemented with intent to cause detriment to the other spouse will thus be – fictitiously – included in the spouses final assets, §1375 II BGB.

§3. THE CLAIM FOR EQUALIZATION

314. The equalization claim amounts to half of the surplus that the other spouse has made in excess of the claiming spouse's surplus (if any). §1378 II BGB limits the amount of this claim to the value of the assets existing at the time of the termination of the property regime. In cases of divorce this may be critical, as the debtor may tactically reduce his assets in the – often considerable – time between the pendency of the application for divorce (as the relevant date for determining the final assets, §1384 BGB) and the actual dissolution, i.e. the day on which the divorce court judgement becomes final, §1564.

315. A spouse's equalization claim may be reduced according to §1380 I BGB if he received assets from the other spouse, either because such dispositions were actually understood to reduce a further equalization claim or because they are presumed to have been meant in such a way because they exceed the value of occasional gifts customary according to the spouses' living conditions.

316. The equalization claim arises upon the termination of the property regime and from this time it is subject to inheritance and transferable, §1378 III 1 BGB.

I. Gross Inequity

317. The debtor may refuse to fulfil an equalization claim partly or entirely if under the circumstances of the individual case an equalization of accrued gains would seem grossly inequitable, *cf.* §1381 BGB. The Courts have been cautious in accepting such gross inequity.[1] They require an intolerable clash with the ideas of justice as in cases where the claimant had significantly and negligently failed to carry out his obligations arising from the conjugal community.[2]

1.   *Cf.* BGH FamRZ 1973, 254.
2.   *See* §1381 II BGB.

II. Contractual Modifications

318. The spouses may – even if they wish to remain under the statutory property regime as such – agree by way of marriage contract (§§1408 I, 1410 BGB) on modifications as to how the equalization of accrued gains is to be conducted in detail. They may thus e.g. exclude certain items of property – e.g. an enterprise – from the equalization. §1378 III 2 BGB also grants the spouses the right to draw up such agreements during the proceedings for the dissolution of their marriage.

§4. Further Claims for Equalization Outside §§1363*sq.* BGB

319. The statutory equalization of surplus under §§1363*sqq.* may not in all cases lead to satisfactory results. Spouses may therefore try and achieve further equalization by way of provisions from outside the marriage law. How far this is possible or whether this is prevented by §1363*sqq.* BGB acting as leges specials in the area of equalization has been subject to debate. It will depend on the grounds that such further claims are based on and may in the individual case pose difficult questions on the interaction of marital property law and general provisions of civil law.

Here it shall suffice to say that the Courts have indeed accepted such further claims, using a restricted notion of 'gifts',[1] or establishing an actual or undisclosed partnership between the spouses.[2]

1.   *Cf.* §§531 II, 812 BGB.
2.   BGHZ 47, 157; BGH FamRZ 1987, 1239.

§5. Special Provisions for Equalization Upon Death

320. In the majority of cases the property regime is terminated by the death of one of the partners. To avoid the complications of the equalization of accrued gains under §§1372 *sqq.* BGB the Code provides for a generalized equalization instead.

321. Where the surviving spouse inherits as the *statutory heir* under §1931 BGB, the surviving spouse's statutory share in the estate will be increased by one quarter of the estate, §1371 I BGB. Where there are relatives of the first degree, e.g. descendants, the spouse will thus be entitled to 1/4 + 1/4 = 1/2 of the estate. The increase will also apply to the compulsory portion, §1371 II BGB.

The addition of one quarter is irrespective of any actual surplus made by the spouses during the marriage in the individual case. An 'equalization' will thus be made even if the marriage lasted only a few days and even if the surviving spouse was actually the one achieving a major surplus in the marriage.

322. Is the surviving spouse the heir by testamentary disposition or where he is the recipient of a legacy, no additional 'equalization' by way of increasing his share is performed as it is assumed that any equalization wanted is already covered by the Will. The spouse may always disclaim the inheritance.

323. Where the surviving spouse does so or where he is neither the heir nor the recipient of a legacy, §1371 BGB does not apply and equalization of accrued gains will be performed according to §§1373 *sqq.* BGB. In addition to that, the spouse may claim the compulsory portion. His suit will be filed against the successors.

Part IV. Succession Law

Chapter 1. Introduction

324. The law of succession is, at presence, of high importance. In so far as the savings of the elder generation have not been destroyed by political or economic catastrophes it is estimated that within the next ten years assets of more than 4.400 Billion DM will be bequeathed to the younger generation, the single estate having a value of more than 300,000 DM on average.

§1. BASIC CONCEPTS OF THE LAW OF INHERITANCE

I. Subject-matter

325. In objective terms the law of succession comprises all norms which regulate the transfer of private proprietary rights and duties on an individual's death. In subjective terms, the law of succession describes the position of a person who has become the heir of another, i.e. the deceased.

II. Legal Sources

326. The Law of Succession is governed by the fifth volume of the German Civil Code (§§1922–2385 BGB) but the other volumes contain provisions partly relating to the Law of Succession as well.

The Law of Succession also appears in the law of heridifary farms (as amended of 26 July 1976) and in International Private Law (Art 25, 26 EGBGB). Even after German reunification, succession in the East before 3 October 1990 is still governed by the Civil Code of the former German Democratic Republic (East Germany) (Art. 235 §1 EGBGB).

If the deceased had his or her assets in both east and west, the estate will be separated.

III. Probate Court Rules

327. The German Civil Code not only contains substantive but also procedural law. That is to say it regulates the competence of the Probate Court, particularly in proceedings for the issue of a certificate of inheritance (§§2353ff). The FGG (law on non-contentious proceedings) contains supplementary regulations in §§72ff.

The rules governing documentation of Wills must also be observed when drawing up notarial Wills and deeds of inheritance.

§2. FUNDAMENTAL PRINCIPLES OF THE LAW OF SUCCESSION

I. Universal Succession

328. The principle of universal succession is the starting point of the German Civil Code. All proprietary rights of the deceased go directly on his death to one or several successors. In contrast to this, strictly personal rights are incapable of being inherited.[1] If several heirs are in existence they will inherit jointly (Joint heirs §2032ff),[2] with the exception of the following: (1) shares in a partnership (OHG, KG); a special type of succession will take place here; (2) Farms inherited according to the law on inheritance of agricultural estates; the farm will also be inherited independently of other assets by its successor.[3]

1. *Cf.* BGHZ 50, 133 'Mephisto'; and in addition Heldrich, *Case 1* and F. Seifert, *Postmortaler Schutz des Persönlichkeitsrechts und Schadensersatz*, NJW 1999, 1889.
2. Paragraphs without references are those of the German Civil Code (BGB).
3. *Cf. Leipold*, in Münchener Kommentar, 3rd ed., 1997, Einl. Rn. 67ff.

II. Succession to Liabilities

329. Inheritance of the total estate and its encumbrances takes place in all assets and liabilities. The heir is therefore liable for the deceased's debts (§1967 BGB), but with the possibility of disclaiming the inheritance (§§1942ff) or opportunity to limit liability (§§1975ff).

III. Bequest of Specific Assets

330. One who is due to receive individual items from the testator's assets in accordance with the Will is termed a specific legatee; he will only have a claim under the law of obligations against the heir or heirs, §2174.

IV. Possible Heir

331. Every individual or legal entity can be an heir irrespective of age and contractual capacity, §1923 I (for practical reasons children who have already been conceived can inherit if they are subsequently born alive according to §1923 II. If a child has not yet been conceived, he can only become a reversionary heir, §2101 I).

V. Entry of Succession

332. Devolution of an inheritance occurs on the death of the decedent, indicated by the stopping of the heart and circulation, but may also occur if the testator has become brain dead.[1]

   1. *Cf. Taupitz*, Um Leben und Tod, JuS 1997, 203, 206.

VI. Intestate Succession

333. Those dying intestate are succeeded by operation of law by their spouse and closest relatives or alternatively, by the State, §§1924ff (*see infra* §2).

VII. Testamentary Succession

334. Notwithstanding this, the decedent can dispose of his assets as he pleases; through the testament and/or deed of succession (§§1937ff) (*see infra* §3). The law will only go so far as to stipulate that a compulsory portion of the estate should go to the surviving spouse and closest relatives. This gives rise to a claim under the law of obligations against the heir or heirs specified in the Will for half of the net worth of the estate (§2303; *see infra* §4).

VIII. Burial

334A. If the descendant has not made provisions by contract with an undertaker or by will, the next skins are entitled to organize the funeral and the grave, irrespective of being an heir.[1]

   1. *Cf.* W. Zimmermann, *Rechtsfragen zum Thema 'Friedhof und Bestattung'*, ZEV 1997, 440.

Chapter 2. Provisions Made and Succession in the Event of Death

§1. INTESTATE SUCCESSION

I. Relatives' Right of Succession

335. In the absence of testamentary provisions made by the deceased, his estate will go to his family by operation of law. Spouses and relatives of the first order are joint heirs. The term relative is determined by §1589 BGB.

A. *System of Parentelic Succession*

336. The order in which relatives have a right to succeed is determined by §§1924ff according to an arrangement that, in essence, favours the younger generations.

1. Primary heirs are the issue of the decedent and their issue. Secondary heirs are the parents of the decedent and their issue (brothers, sisters, nephews, nieces).
   The grandparents and their issue make up tertiary heirs, §1926 I etc. As long as a relative of a higher degree is present, the more distant relative is excluded, §1930.
2. Within the first three degrees a system of *per stir* distribution and lineal heirs applies.
   Each child of the intestate can be a male or female head of a line. His or her issue (grandchildren, great-grandchildren) are related to the intestate via him or her. According to the system of descendants, each descendant receives an equal portion of the inheritance. If the intestate dies as a widower with three children, the three children will inherit equal shares, §1924 IV, even independently of their marital status and whether they have children of their own. Conversely, the lineage describes the relationship of a person to his parents.
3. Each *per stirpital* descendant is represented by the nearest relative ('Principle of Representation') §1924 II. A child will exclude its own children from the line of succession. If that child predeceased the intestate, then his offspring will inherit in his place, §1924 III (termed 'right of pre-emption'). This right of pre-emption continues to apply if the nearer descendant does not become an heir because he disclaims the inheritance for example, is disqualified from receiving it or predeceases the intestate.

B. *Secondary Heirs*

337. Likewise for secondary heirs, succession is still determined by *per stirpital* distribution, the representation principle and right of pre-emption, §1925 BGB. The right to an inheritance according to lineage is more conspicuous when both parents have predeceased the heirs. Half brothers and sisters are related to the intestate via the parents' part and so inherit a portion of half of the parent's part.

C. Tertiary Heirs

338. The tertiary heirs are comprized of the grandparents and their offspring. According to the Principle of Representation, the grandparents inherit if they survive the testator, §1926 II. If they are no longer alive, the right of pre-emption comes into play again, §1926 III. If there are no offspring on the side of one set of grandparents, that portion falls to the other grandparents and to their offspring respectively, §1926 III 2. If one set of grandparents is no longer alive and has no offspring, the other grandparents and their offspring inherit alone, §1926 IV. The offspring's right of pre-emption is determined by the rules governing primary heirs, §1926 V.

D. Further Heirs

339. From the fourth quadiary heirs onward the principle of representation and the right of pre-emption are no longer applicable. All persons who are equally close relatives of the deceased inherit on an equal footing, §1928 II, III, in so far as the great-grandparents are no longer alive.

E. Status of Illegitimate Children

340. Nowadays legitimate and illegitimate children (born after 1 July 1949) inherit in the same way. The Act passed in 1997 dealing with granting equal status to illegitimate children[1] abolished the substituted inheritance right (formerly §1934d) and the claim for advance compensation payments in lieu of future performance (formerly §1934d), both without replacement, for successions taking place after it has come into force (Art. 224 I No.1 EGBGB). The illegitimate child can only validate his right of succession after paternity has been established (§§1594 I, 1600d IV).[2]

1. BGBl 1997 I 2968.
2. As amended by the Child Reform Act 1997, BT Drucks 13/4899 of 12 September 1997.

F. Status of Adopted Children

341. An adopted child becomes a child of the adopting parents and becomes a successor to them according to §§1754, 1924. The relationship with, and along with it, the right to succeed his biological parents is extinguished, §1755. The only exception to this arises when dealing with the adoption of stepchildren, §1756 II. If an adult is adopted, the new relationship is extended only to the adopters and adoptees and the latter's offspring; the relationship to the blood relations remains in existence, §1770.

II. Spouse's Inheritance Rights

342. The spouse is not related to the decedent and therefore his or her right to an inheritance must be subject to special rules. In all legal systems, an effort is made to ensure that provision is made for the surviving spouse after the death of the decedent and to take into account the personal and economic unity of the married couple.

The prerequisite for the spouse's inheritance rights is a valid marriage at the time of death. Even before a divorce decree, the right to an inheritance is extinguished if the deceased applied for the divorce or had agreed to it, §1933, s. 1. The proportion left to the surviving spouse is determined by the matrimonial regime to which the married couple were subject.

A. *Community of Accrued Gain*

343.   1. The spouse inherits a quarter alongside the children according to §1931 I and in addition receives another quarter as a lump sum equalizing accrued gains §§1931 III, 1371 (solution according to the Law of Succession).

Alongside the secondary relatives as well as grandparents, the spouse inherits a half + a quarter = three quarters. If no primary or secondary relatives are available, the surviving spouse will be the sole heir §1931 II; the spouse will also inherit in place of grandparents who have passed away, taking their share §1931 I 2. Afterwards the spouse has a dominant position but must nevertheless share with children and parents and this can lead to difficulties concerning maintenance. Therefore many spouses are against inheriting solely and stipulate that the children should succeed to the deceased's estate first, *cf.* §2269.

2. The spouse's position is strengthened further through the preferential right in respect of the matrimonial household §1932 and the 30 days' maintenance rule §1969 according to which a member of the heir's family also belonging to the household can claim maintenance from the deceased for the first 30 days. The 30 days' maintenance rule is very restricted, however. Extending it to a general claim for maintenance against the estate has also been considered. This could go as far as a full allocation of the estate.

3. Potentially the spouse can improve his or her position by disclaiming the inheritance and claiming the calculated property increment (in accordance with §§1373ff) (property law solution) along with the compulsory portion, §1371 III. The equalization of the accrued gain must then be in excess of 3/7th of the estate if there are children, 2/3rd of the estate if there are secondary heirs. If the spouse does not become the heir or a beneficiary under the Will, he or she can claim the amount calculated to equalize the accrued gains and the compulsory portion out of the share of the inheritance not raised ('small compulsory portion'), §1371 II.[1] According to the opposing view, the spouse can elect to claim the larger compulsory portion (calculated according to a higher

fraction of the inheritance instead of the accrued gain and small compulsory portion) (called the Election Theory). This view is not compatible with the wording of §1371 II and legislative intention.

1.   Named the Unity theory; prevailing opinion, *cf.* Klingelhöffer *ZEV*, 1995, 444.

B. Separation of Property

344. If the couple have agreed upon separation of property through a matrimonial property agreement (§1414) the accrued gain is not equalized and therefore the share of the inheritance is not increased. It remains regulated by §1931 I, II. If the deceased is succeeded by his or her spouse and one or two children, they inherit the whole estate in equal parts, §1931 IV.

The spouse's preferential right (§1932) and the 30 days' maintenance rule remain in existence in their unchanged state.

C. Joint Marital Property

345. If the spouses have a proprietary relationship involving joint marital property by operation of a matrimonial property agreement, the spouse only inherits a quarter of the estate if there are children, a half if there are parents, §1931 I, II. The spouse is provided for by the interest in which he or she holds, independently of interest in the decedent's estate.

1. The decedent's death ends joint marital property. The share of the dead spouse in the joint marital property falls to the estate; his or her inheritance is determined by general rules, §1482.
2. If the surviving spouse is the sole heir, there is no need for a settlement. The joint marital property need only be distributed according to §§1441ff, if there are several heirs. The spouse is entitled to half of the balance after making adjustments for liabilities, §1476 I. The estate, now ready to be allocated, consists of the other half as well as the deceased's special and privileged property, §§1417.
3. Finally, the married couple can arrange continued joint property between the surviving spouse and the children common to them, §1483. Because of the ties connected with it, however, this will happen very rarely even in the case of children who have reached adulthood.

III. The State's Right to Succeed

346. If there is no spouse and there are no relatives in existence, the state becomes the legal heir (§1936). This case also arises when the legal heirs have refused the legacy (e.g. because of excessive debts) or when distant family members cannot be reached (§1964).

The state inherits like a private person. As a result of the function of the fiscal right of succession the state cannot, as the legal heir, refuse to accept the legacy (§1942 II). Exceptionally, the possibility of limiting its liability is always reserved for the state by virtue of the law (§780 II ZPO).

§2. TESTAMENTARY SUCCESSION

I. Testamentary Freedom

A. Constitutional Guarantees

347. Testamentary freedom is an essential component of the German legal system of succession; it is the part of individual autonomy pertaining to the Law of Succession. According to the principle of testamentary freedom, the testator may make dispositions as he pleases in order to exclude or alter legal succession. Testamentary freedom is constitutionally guaranteed through the general freedom principle (Art. 2 I GG), but also through the guaranteed right of succession (Art. 14 I GG).

Testamentary freedom arises in BGB indirectly from §§1937–1941.

The law protects testamentary freedom in §2302. According to it, any contract which obliges someone to make, revoke or not revoke a Will is null and void.

B. No Proxy in Making the Will

348. A disposition *mortis causa* can only be made personally. The testator must make the Will or conclude the contract of inheritance formally and in person, §§2064, 2274. He or she must also personally determine what should be included as regards substantive content.

Following §2065, the testator may not leave the decision to a third party as to whether a disposition *mortis causa* should apply or who should receive specific sums of money. This rule causes problems especially when determining the successor to a business. Therefore in practice the testator is permitted to lay down simply practical criteria for establishing a successor. However, what must be decided then is the identity of the successor, the form in which he should be appointed and the time limit for the person who has to make the final decision to establish a successor.[1]

1. *BGHZ* 15, 199; Ebenroth, Rdn. 185f; R. Zimmermann, *Quos Titius voluerit*, 1991; Heldrich, *Fall 7.*

C. Cancelling of the Will

349. Testamentary freedom is further ensured by the fact that unilateral dispositions *mortis causa* are repealable at any time (§2253). Admittedly, contractual dispositions *mortis causa* do bind the testator; that said, he can always challenge it on the grounds of mistake or undue influence, §2281. Whoever interferes with the testator's testamentary freedom intentionally and unlawfully is not eligible to receive under the Will, §2339 and can be disqualified in an action for nullification (§2342).

D. Illegality of the Will

350. Like every legal transaction, a last Will can be unlawful or immoral and void (§138). It is not permissible, for instance, for a Heimträger or a Heimleiter to allow himself to be a beneficiary of the home's residents (§14 HeimG).[1]

According to the prevailing opinion, immorality is basically determined by the point in time of the undertaking,[2] not the point in time at which the inheritance occurs. A basis of testamentary freedom is the starting point when controlling the content of the last Will. Closest family members are, in principle, protected by the 'compulsory portion'. A Will is only immoral, therefore, when the overall character of the provisions is immoral in terms of content, effects and motive.[3]

The appointment of a lover as heir is therefore only immoral when solely intimate dealings are due to be rewarded through it but not when it appears to be more respectable due to a long-term relationship (house keeping, care when sick, help in a profession, etc.)

What is contentious is whether the testator may favour male issue (the prevailing opinion: yes) and whether marriage clauses or the condition of marrying people of the same class are permissible. The Federal Constitutional Court and the Federal Supreme Court decided in 1999 that such clauses are valid if the testator is persuing reasonable aims with regard to his estate or family traditions.[4]

The Federal Supreme Court also held that a testator may restrict the positions of a handicapped child in favor of it that the public authorities may not recover their nursing expenditures.[5]

1. Rossak, 'Letztwillige Verfügungen von Heimbewohnern zugunsten des Heimträgers oder von Heimmitarbeitern', *ZEV* 1996, 41.
2. BayObLG FamRZ 1997, 656, 661.
3. *Cf.* 'Leipold, Testierfreiheit und Sittenwidrigkeit', in: *50 Jahre BGH. Festgabe aus der Wissenschaft*, Bd. 1, 2000, p. 1011.
4. BVerfG FamRZ 2000, 945; BGHZ 140, 118 = FamRZ 1999, 580; *cf. also* BayObLG FamRZ 1997, 705; OLG Stuttgart FamRZ 1998, 260; Goebel, 'Eheschließungsfreiheit und erbrechtliche Potestativbedingungen', FamRZ 1997, 656.
5. BGHZ 111, 36 = NJW 1990, 2055; BGHZ 123, 368 = NJW 1994, 248; Eichenhofer, 'Das Behindertentestament oder: Sozialhilfe für Vermögende?', *JZ* 1999, 226.

II. The Competency of the Testator to Make a Will

A. Full Capacity

351. A person who has come of age has full testamentary capacity. Also those placed in the care of others to whom consent is reserved, remain competent to make a Will, §1903 II.

B. Capacity of Minors

352. A minor who has turned 16 has restricted testamentary capacity, but can only make a Will by public legacy in the form of an oral declaration or through handing over an open document (§2233 I). The minor cannot create a Will written personally (§2247 IV).

The minor is not competent to make a Will before turning 16 (§2229 I) and cannot make one through a representative as a Will can only be created personally (§2064).

C. General Incapacity

353. Those who lack contractual legal capacity are also incapable of making a Will (§2229 IV). In terms of material, the rule corresponds to §§104 No. 2, 105 II. A Will can later be made effective in a so-called *lucidum intervallum*. In cases of dispute, the court of probate has the task of resolving the issue of the testator's capacity (§§2358 I BGB, 12 FGG). Whoever makes the claim that the testator lacked testamentary capacity carries the burden of proof.[1]

    1.   OLG Hamm FamRZ 1997, 1026.

D. Restrictions for Handicapped

354. Those not able to read can only make a Will through an oral declaration before a notary (§2233 II, 2247 IV). Those not able to speak can only make a Will by handing over a written document (§2233 III). This rule is problematic for those disabled who cannot generally speak comprehensively but because of partial injury or weakness cannot write anymore[1] and accordingly was declared to be void by the Federal Constitutional Court.[2]

A Will which is ineffective at the time of its creation remains null and void, even when the testator becomes legally competent to make a Will later on.

    1.   *Cf.* OLG Hamm FamRZ 1994, 993 with note P. Baumann.
    2.   BVerfG (19 January 1999) FamRZ 1999, 985.

III. Creation and Revocation of a Will

A. Creation

355. A properly constructed Will can only be created with a notary's signature or a hand-written declaration (§2231). In addition to this, an emergency Will can be created in accordance with §2249.

1. Holographic Testament
    A Will written personally by the testator must be written by hand and signed (§2247 I). The deceased must have written the entire text personally. References

to texts which are not written personally by the testator are only permissible in so far as they serve to give a closer explanation of the specific issue, but not to the extent that important provisions are affected. A typed Will which has been signed is invalid. Likewise, a Will which is signed with a facsimile stamp or not signed at all is invalid.[1] The identity of the testator, his earnestness, and that the declaration is final should be ensured through the hand-written draft and signature. The signature should follow along with the Christian names and surnames but can also follow in other ways which are unambiguous (§2247 II). Time and place make establishing the validity easier, but are dispensable when this can be established in other ways (§2247 V).

The Will does not have to be headed as 'a Will' or in similar ways; it is sufficient that the piece of writing contains *earnest provisions* made for the event of death. A letter can also be considered as a personally written Will, if it itself contains the provisions and not simply a portion thereof.

Codicils and additions must always be signed afresh. Writing on top is not sufficient, neither is a signature on a closed envelope under the title 'Will'.

2. The public Will

The testator must declare his intentions for the notary to write down. This is recorded in the form of notary certificates according to the law governing documentation. The Last Will and Testament is regularly declared orally to the notary (after previous discussion and consultation), §2232 S. 1, 2nd case and S. 2. The writing does not need to be written by the testator in any case. It is sufficient that the notary's recording is approved and signed, §13 I BeurkG.

3. Wills made in an emergency

Those finding themselves in acute mortal danger can also make a Will orally before the mayor in the presence of two witnesses, §2249. Those situated in an inaccessible place (at least for the notary), can likewise make a Will orally before the mayor or in cases of acute mortal danger before three witnesses, §2250. The same is possible on board a German ship at sea, §2251. The validity of the Will made in an emergency is restricted to three months duration after its creation (§2252).

1. For a 'blueprint will' *see* Heldrich, case 8.

B. *Revocation of a Will*

356. The Will can basically be revoked at any time, in whole or in part, without justification, §2253. The knowledge of a third party or the promise of the appointment of specific heirs does not prevent the revocation.

Whoever produces a payment on the strength of a promise of subsequent appointment as a future heir, has a claim on the grounds of unjust enrichment in accordance with §812 Sections 1, 2, when the intended result does not occur because he has not become heir. The claim is directed against the testator, after his death against the heirs in the form of a liability of the legacy.[1]

The revocation of the Will results from the making of a new one, §2254, or through the destruction or alteration of the testamentary document with the intention of revocation, §2255. A notary Will is revoked when it is removed from official custody, § 2258. Those creating a new Will revoke the earlier one in so far as it contradicts the former, §2258. If the revocation is revoked, then it is doubtful whether the earlier Will is valid again, §2257. A Will ripped up with the intention that it be revoked does not become valid again merely by sticking it back together.[2]

Since the revocation negates provisions made for the event of death, the testator's legal capacity is required according to §2229. This is also applicable when the testamentary document has been destroyed or retracted from official custody.

On the other hand, a Will is not revoked merely by virtue of the fact that it is ineffectual in reality.

> 1. BGHZ 44, 321.
> 2. BayObLG JuS 1997,172.

C. Challenging the Will

357. If a testator makes a Will on the basis of a mistake, he can correct his error through revoking the Will in so far as he notices it during his lifetime. This being so, the testator does not need to challenge his own Will.

It is different when error or coercion come to light only after the death of the testator. The testator can no longer put his true Will into effect: rather the third party with the right to challenge should be protected from the testator's defective provisions.

A contest on the grounds of mistake or coercion only comes into consideration where the position under the Law of Succession which would correspond to the presumed intention of the testator, cannot be reached through interpretation.

1. Provisions made for the event of death can be challenged in accordance with §§2078, 2079. These extend the right to contest with regard to §§119, 123. Since there is deemed to be no protection for reliance with respect to Wills like there is with contracts, a Will can be contested on the grounds of **any 'mistake of motive'**, according to §2078 II. Along with a challenge on the grounds of mistake, there also appears a challenge on the ground of unlawful threats. Since there can be an appeal against the Will for any mistake as to motive, a challenge on the basis of fraud does not especially need to be admitted.
2. §2079 contains a **special case** of mistake as to motive. According to it, a provision can be challenged when the testator has failed to include those alive on his death who were entitled to a compulsory portion of the Will and whose existence was not known to him on creation of the provisions or those who were just born or became entitled to a compulsory portion after the creation of the provisions.

    There will be no basis for the appeal if it is accepted that the testator would have bequeathed in the same way even if he had been in possession of the full facts, §2079, S. 2.
3. As otherwise, the appeal will result in a **retrospective annulment** of the Will (§142 I). In the case of §2079 it is contentious whether all the provisions are dispensed with or those entitled to a compulsory portion just receive their compulsory portion of the Will whilst others will have their inheritance reduced.[1]

4. **Entitlement to challenge** a Will is, according to §2080, given to those who would be directly entitled to succeed on dissolution of the Last Will and Testament. If several are entitled to challenge, each of them may contest the Will independently. A challenge made by one will be to the benefit of all. In the case of §2079, only those entitled to a compulsory portion can contest the Will (§2080 II), if the error as to content only refers to one specific person who is entitled to challenge the Will, no other person can contest it (§2080 II).

According to §2082 I, the appeal must be made to the court of probate (§2081 I) within one year of the person becoming aware of the grounds for it (§2082 II 1).
   The right of appeal lapses 30 years after the testator's death (§2082 III).

   1.   *Cf.* Ebenroth, Rdn 309; Leipold, Rdn 327.

IV. Contents and Interpretation of Wills

A. Permissible Contents

358. The testator has a wide discretion in organizing his Last Will and Testament as regards content,[1] but must conform to the form dictated by the law of succession. According to it, the Will can contain the following stipulations:

1. the positive appointment of a future heir or heirs to inherit singly or jointly; the negative appointment (or disinheriting) of an heir or heirs, §1938, inheriting before, after and in place of others;
2. individual sums by means of a bequest (§1939, 2147ff) or support (§§1940, 2192ff);
3. requirements/decisions as to how the estate is to be dealt with. Rules about the apportionment of the estate (§§2048, 2049) or the exclusion of differences of opinion (§2044);
4. rules about the compulsory portion;
5. revocation of the previous Will and Testament;
6. decisions relating to family law e.g. appointment of guardians, §1777 III. Restriction of financial support for property given to a child, §1638, declaration as to reserved goods in accordance with §1418 II No. 2.
7. the choice of an indigenous law of succession for property ownership in land, Art. 25 II EGBGB.

   1.   *Cf.* Langenfeld, 'Einführung in die Vertragsgestaltung, Testamente und Erbverträge', *JuS* 1998, 521.

B. Interpretation

359. One of the most frequent disputes in the Law of Succession relates to the correct interpretation of a Will. Privately written Wills are drafted frequently by laymen without legal knowledge and with unorthodox ideas. Problems also arise with the interpretation of notary Wills.[1] The notary can miss the point of a clear recording of a testator's intention; a long period of time can pass between drawing up a Will and death and relationships could have altered to such an extent that it is difficult to derive any sensible meaning from the text under the change of circumstances.

1. Wills are, as unilateral expressions of intention in accordance with §133, as a rule to be interpreted according to the real intention of the deceased. It does not really depend on the position of the recipients or on protecting the expectations of others.

   When in doubt, the words are to be understood as having their general, every day meaning.

   The fundamental basis for interpretation is the benevolent interpretation of a Will, §2084 and is therefore an interpretation which gives practical effect to the provisions.

2. Circumstances external to the Will can also be taken into consideration in the interpretation, if/when they permit conclusions to be drawn about the testator's intention. Admittedly there must be some indication of this intention expressed in the Will (the intimation theory) because otherwise the rules determining the form of the Will could be undermined.

3. If the state of affairs has changed between death and drawing up the Will in a way not contemplated by the testator, then it must be checked whether the gap in the Will can be closed in a way which does not amend the interpretation. The aim is to realize the intentions of the testator, in as far as possible. It must also be asked what the testator would have wanted if he had also considered the intermediate event. There it can concern either the beneficiary or the object being bequeathed. Supplementing by means of a hypothetical intention from the Will must follow. According to the prevailing opinion, the Will must contain some kind of evidence to suggest that the change would have been acceptable to the testator and this will depend namely on the hypothetical intention of the testator at the time of the drawing up of the Will.

   The new interpretation will also come under consideration (§140), if a provision which is void can have its meaning changed to make it into an valid one.

4. Legal rules for interpretation

   a) Appointment of a future heir. Laymen use the terms 'inheriting' and 'bequeathing' as synonyms or wholly non-technical terms. Whether someone is appointed as future heir is not determined by the way the testator has expressed himself, but exclusively according to the content of the Last Will and Testament. Whoever is bequeathed the estate in its entirety or just a fraction thereof is an heir;[2] whoever is bequeathed individual objects is, in doubtful cases, a non-heir, §2087. If the testator completely divides his estate into different groups of objects, the beneficiaries could be joint heirs with a division arrangement (§2048).

   b) Doubts as to the beneficiary. §§2066ff contain various, more or less important rules in the event of doubt as to the beneficiary. Whoever appoints his future legal heir in indefinite terms has, in case of doubt, appointed those who are the statutory heirs at the time of the testator's death, §2066. Whoever appoints his children or offspring who then die, is deemed, if in doubt, to have appointed his grandchildren, §§2068, 2069, likewise also those born after the death.[3] If the testator has named his spouse as a beneficiary, then the provision is nullified in cases of doubt if the marriage was void or was dissolved by the testator, §2077.[4] A final heir is, in doubt, also a substitute heir.[5] If the spouse is named in life assurance on the death of his/her partner as a beneficiary, the right will not be extinguished on divorce so long as it is not revoked as regards that insurance (§166 II VVG). In the relationship between the spouses, however, the basis for the transaction for the bequest is negated. Hence the heirs can seize that money held by the surviving ex-spouse, provided that it is not apparent from the intention of the testator that the former spouse should keep the insurance money.

c) Lack of clarity about the size of the portion of the inheritance. §§2088ff contain rules for the procedure when, in a Will, some of the estate has not been allocated or is over-allocated or the inheritance portions are imprecise.

If the testator has excluded intestate succession by appointing several heirs, intestate succession will not occur on the losing of one of the chosen heirs; the portion of the inheritance of those lost will be used to increase the remaining ones proportionally, §2094 I 1. Admittedly, the increase is ruled out when the testator has directly appointed a replacement heir, §2099 or it can be interpreted as such (especially in accordance with §2069).

d) Interpretation of Conditions, *cf.* §§2074, 2075.

1. *Cf.* BayObLG FamRZ 1997, 1243.
2. *Cf.* BayObLG FamRZ 1997, 1242.
3. OLG Cologne JuS 1993, 163.
4. Through marrying again the provision does not become operative again, BayObLG NJW 1996, 133.
5. OLG Frankfurt JuS 1996, 557.

V. The Joint Will of Spouses

A. *The Object of a Joint Will*

360. A full life spent with someone frequently results in the wish to regulate the financial position after the death of the first and second spouse through mutually agreed provisions suited to each partner. The law accommodates this practical need in two ways:

1. It makes the form of a joint Will simpler; and
2. in the case of provisions, the subject of which changes, whoever of the two lives longer is compelled to accept the provisions of the other partner who predeceases him. The practical result of this is that a joint Will arises for the death of both spouses. In practice, the joint Will is of great significance.

B. The Creation of a Joint Will

361. 1. Only spouses can create a joint Will, §2265. While engaged couples can make a pre-nuptial agreement and contract of inheritance before marriage which comes into effect afterwards, §§1408 I, 2274, 2275 III, a joint Will can only be created after a valid marriage.

2. A joint testament can be created by a notary or as a privately written Will. Since the spouses create the Will jointly, each spouse must be aware of the provisions of the other.

   In practice, personally written Wills are created most frequently. For them, §2667 allows for a simplification of their form. It is sufficient for one spouse to write the Will and sign it and for the other spouse simply to sign it personally along with him or her.

3. The joint character of the Will's creation can also arise out of other circumstances, for example out of mutual provisions in the same piece of writing under opposite reference, which refer to each other etc.

C. Contents of the Joint Will

362. 1. The married couple can make Wills independently of each other in the same joint testament.

2. The mutual provisions can also be legally dependent upon each other, if they are reciprocal provisions, §2270 I. Whether this is the case is to be established with individual interpretation.[1]

   Interdependency is to be assumed according to the rules of interpretation in §2270 II:
   a) when each of the spouses remembers the other in his or her Will (as heirs, beneficiaries, etc.) or
   b) when a spouse makes a financial contribution to the other and this provides, in the case of his survival, for the benefit of a third party who is related or close to the receiving spouse.[2]
   The third party can, but does not have to be related to the other spouse. In contrast to this, when in doubt a change of beneficiary cannot be accepted, if the surviving person only provides for those related or close to him. If spouses remember each other and stipulate that after the death of the surviving spouse the mutual legacy should fall to their children, then it cannot be said that each spouse remembers their children because the other does so.[3]

   Interdependency has significant legal consequences:
   a) If a joint and mutual Will is void or repealed, the other spouse's provisions are also ineffective (§2270 I). This legal consequence applies to the appointment of future heirs, to bequests, and conditions, according to §2270 III. Other provisions, like naming an executor, arrangements as to how to divide the estate, disinheriting a relative or the withdrawing of a compulsory portion still remain valid on the

provision of the other spouse becoming void, in so far as the existence of the other's provisions is not promoted to a condition relating to how the valid Will should be arranged.

If a joint Will also contains unilateral provisions along with interdependent provisions, then the nullity of the interdependent provisions will result in the rest becoming void only when it is accepted that the unilateral provisions would be unaffected without those of interdependent content, §2085.

b) An interdependent joint Will cannot be repealed during the other's life through unilateral provision, §2271 I 2. A repeal is only possible as it would be in rescission of a contract of inheritance, i.e. through communication to the other spouse and, to be more exact, in notorially documented form, §2271 I 1 i.V.m. §2296 II.

c) On the death of the other spouse, the right to revoke is extinguished; the surviving partner can only repeal his own dispositions if he refuses things bequeathed to him §2271 II 1. The only exception to this is where the surviving spouse would be authorized to amend or repeal the testament (reserved right of amendment or exemption clause).

d) A binding joint and mutual Will does not prevent the disposal of the property during the lives of the parties. This is laid down expressly for contracts of inheritance §2286, but also applies correspondingly to joint Wills. Only in the case of gifts made with the intention of interfering with the Will does the heir affected have a claim for restitution against the beneficiary analogous to §2287.

3. Spouses appoint each other frequently as future heirs and determine that after the death of the last to die the children should receive the property. Legally the end result can be achieved in 2 ways:

a) The surviving spouse becomes the provisional heir of whichever partner dies first, the children the reversionary heir of the first to die and the full heir of the last parent to die ('The Separation Principle' as it is called';)[4] or,

b) The surviving spouse alone becomes the full heir of the first to die, the children become the heirs of the parent who dies afterwards but are excluded from succeeding after the first to die (the Unity Principle; Berlin Testament). In accordance with the legal rules of interpretation in §2269, the Unity Principle applies when in doubt. The disadvantage of this construction is that the children can demand the compulsory portion on the death of the first testator, §2303. In order to avoid this, it is common practice to dictate that a child who demands the compulsory portion on the event of the death of the first testator should be excluded from the final succession.

4. A remarriage clause can frequently be found in joint Wills, according to which the surviving spouse must give the legacy to the children in the event of remarrying. In cases of doubt this means that the full inheritance of the survivor is conditionally annulled (§§158 II, 2075) and at

the same time a provisional and reversionary heir is arranged but conditionally postponed. Only on the death of the surviving spouse is it firmly decided whether he has become the full heir or not.[5] According to the opposing view, the survivor must have regard to his commitments as a provisional heir who has been freed so long as he can marry. Therefore it treats him as a conditionally annulled provisional heir combined with a conditionally postponed position of provisional heir.[6]

1. For the individual cases *cf.* Pfeiffer, 'Das gemeinschaftliche Ehegattentestament', *FamRZ* 1993, 1266.
2. *See* BayObLG FamRZ 1997, 1241; Ratke, *Die Darstellung des Berliner Testaments und der gegenseitigen gemeinschaftlichen Einsetzung der Ehegatten zu Vorerben*, 1999.
3. BayObLG FamRZ 1985, 1287; *cf. also* Heinrich JuS 1995, 631.
4. *Cf.* BayObLG FamRZ 1997, 1241f.
5. Cf. BGHZ 96, 198.
6. *Cf.* MünchKomm/*Musielak*, 3rd ed., 1997, §2269 Rdn. 54ff, but who agrees with the conclusions of the prevailing opinion.

D. *Challenging a Joint Will*

363. In so far as a interdependent joint Will has become binding after the death of a spouse, the surviving spouse must be able to absolve himself by submitting grounds for objection. The question is only legally regulated in the case of a contract of inheritance. Analogous to §§2281 ff the surviving spouse can challenge[1] the former joint Will, in particular after remarrying again.[2]

1. *Leipold*, Rdn 355; *Ebenroth*, Rdn. 299; *cf.* BayObLG FamRZ 1995, 1024 = JuS 1996, 76; Dohr, 'Überwindung der aufgrund gemeinschaftlichen Testaments oder Erbvertrages entstandenen erbrechtlichen Bindung', MittRhNotK 1998, 381–419.
2. *See* J. Ritter, *Der Konflikt zwischen einer erbrechtlichen Bindung aus erster Ehe und einer Verfügung des überlebenden Ehegatten zugunsten eines neuen Ehepartners*, 1999.

VI. The Contract of Inheritance

A. *Admissibility*

364. The testator can dispose of his assets *mortis causa* by contractual means, §§2274ff. This contract has only the effect of a disposition *mortis causa* but binds the testator with the result that the directions stipulated in the contract can no longer be unilaterally revoked, §2289 I. The purpose of the contract of inheritance is to bring about this commitment, mostly in the interests of the other contractual partner because the testator expects to be provided with some kind of services or that the partner makes some desirable decision and the estate is being used as valuable consideration.[1]

The contract of inheritance is a regular contract. To protect the testator from contracting it in haste, it must be recorded by a notary, §2276.

The testator is bound by the provisions as stipulated by the contract, but can dispose of his wealth freely during his lifetime, in so far he does not make gifts in bad faith, §§2286ff. The person due to inherit under the contract, therefore, has no legally ensured future interest in an estate of a specific size but only a factual prospect of acquisition. This cannot be ensured through registration.

1. *Cf.* A. Poser, *Der entgeltliche Erbvertrag im Zivil- und Steuerrecht*, 2000.

B. Concluding a Contract of Inheritance

365. The testator can only conclude a contract of inheritance personally, §2274 and, namely, by having it authenticated by a notary; for this, both contractual parties must be present before the notary simultaneously, §2276.

Since the contract of inheritance is a contract, the rules governing general capacity to contract will apply, §2275 I.

C. Contents of the Contract of Inheritance

366. 1. In a contract of inheritance future heirs may be appointed, bequests made and conditions laid down by contractual means; other dispositions remain unilateral, §2278. A contractual obligation exists only to such an extent that a obligation has been agreed expressly or the will of the two parties can be determined by interpretation. For contractual regulations, the rules on bequests apply correspondingly, §2279 I. Only the rules on challenging a Will fail to apply.

The contract of inheritance can also contain unilateral dispositions; in so far as a general right to make a Will is applicable, §2299.

2. The contents of a contract of inheritance may vary things. One or both contractual parties can make a Will; they can also appoint each other as beneficiaries. Several people can also conclude a contract of inheritance with each other.

In the case of a bilateral contract of inheritance the nullity of a reciprocal disposition will result in the other becoming void, §2298. A **provisional withdrawal** will also lead to the revocation of the entire contract, §2298 II 1.

3. The contract of inheritance can be concluded (mostly) with or without consideration. As a rule, the appointment of a future heir serves to ensure the past or future performance of the other contractual party. Admittedly it does not involve a reciprocal agreement. If the duty to maintain or care for the opposite side is repealed before the death of the testator, **then it can be admitted via a contractual disposition**, §2295.

D. Obligations Arising from a Contract of Inheritance and their Removal

367. 1. On concluding the contract of inheritance the testator is committed to his contractual dispositions *mortis causa*. Earlier Wills are repealed in so far as they **impair the** rights of the contractual beneficiaries, §2289. Later dispositions will also be invalid to the same extent, §2289 I 2. This will also cover any legal or economic infringement of any of the contractual heirs' rights. A disposition of this nature can only be valid with the consent of the other contractual partner, **which requires the form of a contract of rescission**, §2290.

2. The contract of inheritance (like other contracts) can also lack a beneficiary because of his death, his exclusion or because someone has been disqualified from receiving under the Will. In such cases a disposition made earlier or later will be valid.

3. Otherwise the testator can basically dispose of his assets only in so far as a right to change has been reserved.

4. The effect of the obligation can be extinguished:
   a) through mutual consent, §2290, in the form of a contract of inheritance, §2290 IV. Spouses can also revoke a contract of inheritance through a joint Will, §2292.
   b) After the death of the other contractual party the contract of inheritance can no longer be revoked, §2290 I 2. A third party due to benefit under the contract of inheritance cannot therefore conclude a contract to revoke the first, but may simply declare his intention to waive the inheritance, §§2348, 2350.
   c) Exceptionally, bequests made contractually can be repealed through a simple Will with the consent of the other contractual partner; the declaration of consent then needs to be recorded by a notary, §2291.
   d) The testator can declare that he is rescinding the contract of inheritance:[1]
      i) on reserving the right to withdraw, §2293,
      ii) on serious misdemeanours of the beneficiary, §2294 and
      iii) on revocation of the corresponding obligations of the other party. In each case the declaration of rescission is to be made to the other contractual party and recorded by a notary §2296 II. If the testator is entitled to rescind, then he can do so through a Will after the death of the other contracting party, §2297.
   e) Finally the testator can challenge the contractual dispositions in accordance with the requirements of §§2281. The challenge must be made personally, requires official authentication, and must be declared within a year of becoming aware of the grounds for challenge. As long as the other contractual party is alive, the challenge is to be declared to him, §143 II. After the death of the contractual partner the disposition in question for the benefit of a third party can be challenged in the probate court, §2281 II.

5. **Consequences.** If the contract of inheritance is rescinded, any unilateral dispositions will become null and void if in doubt, §2299 III. As a rule the consequences of the legal rescission are confined to the obligation which is the cause of the rescission; the preservation of other interests is judged according to §§2279, 2085; it therefore depends on whether the remaining dispositions would have been made independently.

In the case of a bilateral contract of inheritance the whole contract is annulled on rescission, §2298 II 1. Annulling the contract by challenging it will cause the contractual dispositions to become invalid in the same way, §2298 I.

6. The contract of inheritance will only lead to an obligation in terms of dispositions *mortis causa*. Through a legal transaction *inter vivos* the testator can, in contrast to this, dispose of his assets freely, §2286. Only gifts made with the intention of interfering with the Will can be drawn on; the beneficiary can demand the gift from the recipients according to the law of restitution, §2287. The term 'gift' takes its meaning from §516. The unnamed donations between spouses as they are known are, within the scope of §2287, to be treated as gifts.[2] An intention to interfere can only be shown to arise when there is no significant personal interest evident in the testator making the donation. The intention to interfere with the rights of the contractual heirs does not have to be the main impetus for the gift.[3]

1. *Cf.* Dohr, 'Überwindung der aufgrund gemeinschaftlichen Testaments oder Erbvertrages entstandenen erbrechtlichen Bindung', MittRhNotK 1998, 381.
2. BGHZ 116, 167 = NJW 1992, 564.
3. BGHZ 59, 343.

§3. THE RIGHT TO A COMPULSORY PORTION

368. In accordance with the principle of testamentary freedom the testator can also disinherit his relatives. The right to a compulsory portion secures a minimum share in the estate for the closest relatives. This statutory reserve is in line with the constitutional guarantee of free testamentary disposition.[1] According to German law, those entitled to a compulsory portion are not substantive 'legitimate heirs' but only have a claim for a share against the heirs based on the law of obligations; the claim for the compulsory portion is an estate liability (§1967 II).

1. *Cf.* Haas, 'Ist das Pflichtteilsrecht verfassungswidrig?', ZEV 2000, 249; B Dauner-Lieb, 'Das Pflichtteilsrecht', *Forum Familien- und Erbrecht* 2000, 110; Schlüter, 'Die Änderung der Rolle des Pflichtteilsrechts, in: *50 Jahre BGH. Festgabe der Wissenschaft.* Bd. 1, 2000, p. 1047; Henrich, *Testierfreiheit vs. Pflichtteilsrecht,* 2000.

I. The Compulsory Portion

A. *Entitled Persons*

369. Those entitled to a compulsory portion are the descendants, the parents and the spouse, not siblings however, §2303. Distant descendants and parents are not entitled to a compulsory portion, in so far as a descendant who takes precedence can claim the compulsory portion or can accept what has been left to him, §2309.[1]

Those entitled to a compulsory portion must be completely excluded from succession to the estate by the disposition *mortis causa*. Whoever turns down the inheritance will only have a claim for the compulsory portion in cases under §§2306 I 2 and 2303 II 2, 1371 III. In contrast to this, a beneficiary excluded from the Will can always claim the compulsory portion, §2307.

1. In addition Bestelmeyer, 'Das Pflichtteilsrecht der entfernten Abkömmlinge', *FamRZ* 1997, 1124.

B. Debtor of the Legal Portion

370. The heir is the debtor of the compulsory portion, §2303 I 1. Several heirs are liable as joint debtors, §2058ff. After the estate has been apportioned, a co-heir who is himself entitled to a compulsory portion can refuse to pay others in satisfaction of their right to a compulsory portion, in order that he keeps his own compulsory portion, §2319.

C. Extent of the Legal Portion

371. The compulsory portion amounts to half of the value of the intestate share, §2303 I 2. When calculating this share those who are disclaiming or rejecting their inheritance should be included, §2310. The decisive factor is the value of the legacy at the time of succession, §2311. Since those entitled to a compulsory portion have no knowledge of the size of the estate, they can demand information from the heirs, §2314 I 1.

D. Donations to be Set off Against the Legal Portion

372. If the testator has made a payment during his lifetime to set off against the compulsory portion, then this will be binding on the claim of those involved, §2315. Likewise, the legal obligation to offset the *losses* of descendants following §§2050ff or §2057a are to be included in the calculation of the compulsory portion.

II. Protection of the Compulsory Portion

373. The compulsory portion should ensure a minimum share in the estate for those entitled to it. If, considered in economic terms, the testator has left those entitled to the compulsory portion with less than this, they can make supplementary claims or demand release from liabilities with the end result being that they are due the compulsory portion at the very least.

A. The Claim for the Remainder of the Compulsory Portion

374. If those entitled to a compulsory portion are left a share of the inheritance that is less than half of the intestate share, then they can make a residual claim to the extent of the difference between the two sums, §2305. Those entitled can not reject the inheritance and claim the full compulsory portion instead.

B. Protection from Liabilities

375. If a share of an inheritance is limited through bequest, a charge, the appointment of a reversionary heir or other things of this nature with the result that the share left to him is equal to or less than the compulsory portion, the liabilities and constraints are invalid §2306 I 1.[1] In addition to this, a claim for the rest of the compulsory portion can be brought if necessary. If the share of the inheritance left to him is bigger than that, the person entitled to the compulsory portion can choose whether he wants to live with the constraint; he can, however, also reject the Will and claim the compulsory portion, §2306 I 2. If a person entitled to a compulsory portion is bequeathed only a testamentary gift, falling short of the compulsory portion, then he can reject this and instead claim the full compulsory portion, §2307 I 1. If he does not reject the bequest he must let its value be deducted from his compulsory portion, §2307 I 2. A spouse who lived under the statutory matrimonial property regime of the community of surplus restricted to property acquired after the marriage ('Zugewinngemeinschaft') can, if he or she accepts the bequest, claim the full compulsory portion (according to increased share of the inheritance); if he or she disclaims the bequest, then he or she can only claim the small compulsory portion and what would be calculated to equalize the accrued gains.

1. *Cf.* BGH NJW 1993, 967.

C. Right to a Supplement to the Compulsory Portion

376. 1. In practice, the testator could undermine the claims for compulsory portions by giving away a substantial part of his assets during his lifetime. It is against this that those entitled to a compulsory portion should be protected. The right to a supplement to the compulsory portion is determined by the amount by which the compulsory portion is raised when the gifts made in the last ten years which must be used as supplements are included in the calculation of the total estate, §2325 I. It is not compulsory for a gift in discharge of a moral debt to be included, §2330. The concept of a gift can be understood to take its meaning from §516 I. In the case of mixed donations, the part not considered to be remuneration must be included in the adjustments.[1] Donations that go back ten years remain unaffected with the exception of gifts made to the spouse of the testator, §2325 III.

2. The right to have one's compulsory portion supplemented is independent of the claim for the compulsory portion itself. The only prerequisite is that the person making the claim should theoretically be entitled to a compulsory portion. This supplement to the compulsory portion can also only be demanded when more than the compulsory portion

was donated, the surplus value of the estate remaining behind after the claim to a supplement, §2326, S. 2.[2] A supplement can only be claimed by those already entitled to do so when the donation was carried out.[3] Whoever becomes entitled to a compulsory portion (e.g. through marriage) can only after the donation is made use the estate that the testator had at this point in time as his or her basis.

3. The main person held to account for the claim for a supplement is the heir. If he himself is entitled to a compulsory portion, he can refuse the right to a supplement so that the supplemented compulsory portion remains with him, §2328.

The recipient of the gift is only secondarily liable, i.e. in so far as the heir is not obliged to supplement the compulsory portion, §2329. The sole heir can also claim a supplement to his compulsory portion, §2329 I 2.

1. *See* Pentz, 'Pflichtteilsergänzung bei "gemischten" Schenkungen', FamRZ 1997, 724.
2. *Cf.* C. Steiner, 'Pflichtteilsergänzung auch für den 'nicht enterbten' Pflichtteilsberechtigten', MDR 1997, 906.
3. BGH NJW 1997, 2676.

III. Exclusion of the Compulsory Portion

A. *Loss of the Right to Inherit*

377. Those who have been disqualified from receiving under a Will or who have waived their right to inherit[1] have no right to a compulsory portion, §§2345 II, 2346 I 2. The waiver of a right to inherit can also be confined to the compulsory portion, §2346 II. Such a renunciation can only be arranged during the lifetime of the testator.[2]

1. Cf. OLG Frankfurt JuS 1996, 1133
2. BGH NJW 1997, 521.

B. *Divestment of the Compulsory Portion*

378. A breakdown in family relations between the testator and the person entitled to a compulsory portion due to serious crimes on the part of the latter gives the testator the right to withdraw the compulsory portion in his last Will, §§2333ff, 2336.[1] The removal of the compulsory portion extends to all the claims for it; it also contains a disinheritance.

1. *Cf.* OLG Düsseldorf JuS 1996, 751.

C. *The* bona fide *Confinement of the Compulsory Portion*

379. The testator can limit the right to a compulsory portion for a wasteful descendant or a descendant with too many debts by appointing the issue of the descendants as reversionary heirs or reversionary legatees; an administrative executor can also be appointed.[1]

1. §2338; W. Baumann, 'Die Pflichtteilsbeschränkung in guter Absicht', ZEV 1996, 121.

D. Statutory Bars

380. The claim for a compulsory portion becomes statute-barred three years after the discovery of the disposition which infringes their rights by those entitled to inherit and after 30 years at the latest, §2332.

E. Delay in Paying out the Compulsory Portion

381. An heir who is himself entitled to a compulsory portion can claim a deferment in the payment of the compulsory portion in order to avoid unusual hardship, §2331a.

§4. LEGAL TRANSACTIONS ON SUCCESSION

I. Power of Agency

382. Since the power of agency on the death of the grantor basically cannot be extinguished, §§168 S. 1, 672 S. 1, the testator can make provisions that after his death his estate is to be dealt with and business with banks and insurance incapable of being postponed can be carried out, without the heirs having to be investigated or granted a certificate of inheritance. The power of agency, postponed on condition of the agency grantor's death, can then be granted as a postmortem authorization. The authorized does not need to wait for any instructions from the heirs; his competence is limited, however, by the rules on the misuse of the power of agency.[1]

After the death of the testator the agent represents the heir or heirs so that each heir can revoke the agency in place of himself; the executor and the estate administrator can revoke likewise.[2]

1. *Cf.* Trapp ZEV 1995, 314; Seif, 'Die postmortale Vollmacht', AcP 200 (2000), 192; Werkmüller, *Vollmacht und Testamentsvollstreckung als Instrumente der Nachfolgegestaltung bei Bankkonten*, ZEV 2000, 305.
2. *Cf.* Palandt/Edenhofer, 59. ed. 2000, Einf. Vor §2197, Rdn. 16ff.

II. Donations on Succession

A. Form of Promises mortis causa

383. A promise to make a gift on death is only valid if it is carried out by means of a disposition *mortis causa*, §2301 I 1.

B. *Donations Executed* inter vivos

384. An *inter vivos* gift is, in contrast, valid in accordance with the general rules on gifts, §2301 II. This means, above all, that on execution, an informal gift is effective, §518 II.

1. The gift is only then executed when the donor has already directly reduced his estate in his lifetime. It is sufficient for the beneficiary to receive a future interest *in rem*, which protects him from its unilateral withdrawal by the donor. It does not suffice as an execution for the testator to empower the beneficiary to appropriate the object in question on his death.[1]
2. If the donor introduces/instates a third party, then it is not a requirement that the effect of the execution has already fully arisen at the time of death. According to the prevailing opinion it is sufficient that the beneficiary has attained a future interest in the sense that he can receive the donated object without the donor acting any further by way of performance.

It is sufficient for the third party to carry out the first necessary act of execution after the death of the donor.[2] The representative can no longer make the necessary declarations if the heirs have revoked the mandate or authority beforehand.[3]

1. BGHZ 87, 19.
2. According to the prevailing opinion, *cf.* MünchKomm/Musielak, §2301 Rdn. 24ff; a.A. RGZ 83, 223 – Bonifazius-Fall.
3. *Cf. also* BGH NJW 1995, 953; with note Habersack JuS 1996, 585.

III. The Contract for the Benefit of a Third Party Effective on Death

A. *Admissibility*

385. §§328, 331 provide expressly that performance towards a third party on the death of the promisee can be stipulated by contract. By virtue of the contract, the third party receives the claim from the promisee and not from the legacy. The most frequent application of this is the capital life insurance on death. Arrangements with banks, by which the testator leaves claims to a third party from a savings agreement or securities deposit contract, also have practical significance.

In 'cover ratio' the relationship between the contracting parties follows the normal contractual rules.

B. *Covering Relation Between Testator and Beneficiary*

386. It is contentious whether the donation by the testator to the third party beneficiary must be made in the form of a testament and whether accordingly the form requirements contained in §2301 are to be adhered to.[1] According to the prevailing opinion it concerns a gift between living persons; the lack of registration of an intention to make a gift, according to §518 II, becomes irrelevant on the death of the testator. If the beneficiary does not know of his good fortune, the gift can be arranged after the death of the testator. In that case the insurer or the bank passes the offer of a gift, which is also valid after the testator's death (§§672, 130 II),[2] on to the beneficiary; he can accept it without declaring it to the heirs (§§153, 151). Nevertheless the heirs can prevent the contract to make a gift coming into existence by a rapid revocation of the bank's mandate.[3]

1. For this Kipp/Coing, §81 IV, V; Harder, Rdn. 515ff.
2. But *see* M. Janko, *Die bewusste Zugangsverzögerung auf den Todesfall*, 2000.
3. BGH NJW 1975, 382; but *see* G. Vollkommer, 'Erbrechtliche Gestaltung des Valutaverhältnisses beim Vertrag zugunsten Dritter auf den Todesfall?', ZEV 2000, 10.

IV. Succession Clauses in Partnership Contracts

A. *Consequences of Death of Partner*

387. Partnership under the German Civil Code is dissolved on the death of a partner, if nothing else has been agreed in the partnership contract, §727 I. Since the commercial law reform of 1998 this rule is no longer valid for the general partnership and the limited paretnership; here the partnership now remains in existence, unless the dissolution is not agreed upon in the contract. The deceased partner is excluded, thus the compensation only is part of the estate.

B. *Continuation Clauses*

388. The partners can agree that the company should remain in existence among the remaining partners (*cf.* §138 HGB). A possible claim for a lump-sum settlement (§738 BGB) falls to the legacy.

C. *Succession Clauses*

389. A continuation can also be agreed with the heir or heirs of the deceased. According to prevailing opinion, each heir becomes a partner who, according to the succession clause, and on account of their right to inherit have become the successor to the testator. A purely company law succession clause will be refused because of the liability for debts that comes with it; a non-heir can therefore only be given an option to enter into the partnership (partnership agreement as a contract for the benefit of a third party).[1]

Because of the liability structure of the company, the co-heirs each receive an independent part of the original share of the deceased in the company in so far as there is no joint property in the original share ('special succession').

1. BGHZ 68, 255 = NJW 1977, 1339. *Cf.* Dauner-Lieb, *Erbrechtlich und Gesellschaftrechtliche Probleme der Unternehmensnachfolge*, Forum Familien- und Erbrecht 1999, 36.

D. Qualified Succession Clauses

390. If the company is to be continued with only one or a single heir, only those in question become partner on the testator's death.[1]

a) If in doubt it is to be accepted that all of the testator's share in the company should fall to the successor.[2] The share in the company belongs to the estate, at least in terms of value, and also with regard to the liability for the debts of the estate.

b) If a co-heir receives more from the estate through his share in the company than he is due on the grounds of his share as a joint heir, he is obliged to compensate the other co-heirs.[3] However, the testator can exclude this obligation to reduce the share and compensate the other co-heirs within the limits of the right to a compulsory portion.[4]

1. *Cf.* Heldrich, case 2.
2. BGHZ 68, 225.
3. BGHZ 68, 225.
4. MünchKomm/Dütz, §2032 Rdn. 54; MünchKomm/Ulmer, §727 Rdn. 35.

Chapter 3. The Legal Position of the Heir

§1. DEVOLUTION OF THE INHERITANCE AND LEGAL POSITION OF THE HEIR

I. Devolution of the Inheritance, Waiver and Acceptance

A. *Autonomic Transfer of Ownership*

391. According to German law the heir receives the inheritance immediately and directly on the death of the testator, §1922; by virtue of the law he becomes the owner of the estate, §857. In contrast, an heir in Austria will only receive after a allocation through the court of probate. In Common Law countries the estate goes to the personal representative first of all; he has the estate liabilities to pay and only then can he distribute the net estate to the heir or heirs. In German Law the regulation of the estate liabilities is, in contrast, the duty of the heir himself; he can avoid these by waiving the inheritance.

B. *Waiver of the Inheritance*

392. 1. According to German Law one can become the heir automatically, but can turn down the inheritance and as a result annul the devolution, §1953 I. The reason for the waiver is often that the estate has excessive debts. But it can also serve to let the inheritance be distributed to whoever would have been named as the heir, if the person who turned down the inheritance had not been the successor, §1953 II.
2. The waiver must follow within six weeks of discovering the succession and legal basis for his appointment, §1944, through declaration to a court of probate, §1945. The repudiation cannot take place until after the testators death, §1946. The inheritance can also be waived before the testator's death through a contract with the testator, §§2346ff.

   The court of probate has the task of informing the next in line of the repudiation, §1953 III. For this there is a six-week deadline by which the inheritance must be turned down, §1944, by the next in line.
3. The heir cannot repudiate the legacy once he has accepted it. The acceptance can be made expressly or by implication to the creditors of the estate or to the court of probate (application for the grant of a certificate of inheritance, disposal of items belonging to the estate). The inheritance is also accepted when the deadline for disclaiming the inheritance has passed, §1943, 2.
4. If an inheritance is accepted or rejected by mistake, this declaration can be rescinded according to §§119, 123. Contesting on the grounds of mistake as to the contents of the legacy (§119 II) is important. Mistake as to future political and legal developments, for instance the continued existence of the German Democratic Republic (East Germany) and the

depreciation of assets located there, does not result in an entitlement to contest the Will.[1]

So that the legal position does not remain undecided for too long, acceptances and rejections can only be contested within six weeks from learning of the grounds for challenge or from the point at which the coercion is no longer present, §1954. Contesting the acceptance is considered a rejection of the Will, and contesting the rejection counts as an acceptance, §1957 I. Contesting therefore annuls (in contrast to §142 I) not only the former declaration but simultaneously contains the opposite declaration as well; a new period for consideration is not permitted.

1. *Cf.* Grunewald, 'Die Auswirkungen eines Irrtums über politische Entwicklungen in der DDR auf Testamente und Erbausschlagungen', NJW 1991, 1208.

C. The Legal Position of the Provisional Heir

393. 1. The provisional heir is the owner of the estate from its devolution, §1922 I, and can dispose of it. If he turns down the inheritance later on, his dispositions are considered to have been made by someone not entitled to make them, but can be valid according to §932. On waiving the inheritance the estate will go retrospectively to the heirs instated at this point; but the items/objects disposed of will be lost because the provisional heir was the real and rightful owner at the time of the disposal.[1] Urgent dispositions of the provisional heir are always valid irrespective of the good faith of those acquiring them §1959 III. Transactions that must be undertaken in relation to the heir (e.g. the termination of a lease), also remain valid after the Will is rejected, §1959 III.
   2. The provisional heir is also liable for the debts of the estate, §1967 I. These can not be legally validated against him before his acceptance, §1958. Before acceptance, it is permissible to enforce a title against the testator from within the estate only and not against the personal assets of the heir, §778 I ZPO. Personal creditors of the heir are not permitted to enforce against the estate, §778 II ZPO. A creditor who wishes to enforce his rights when the issue is still pending must apply to the court of probate for an order to appoint a provisional administrator, §§1960, 1961.
   3. If the provisional heir has carried out some dealings before rejecting the inheritance then he is to be treated as a *negotiorum gestor* (person performing a service for or acting on behalf of another without authority to do so) in relation to the final heir, §1959 I.

1. Prevailing opinion; Leipold, Rdn. 453; Ebenroth, Rdn. 350.

II. Disqualification from Succession

394. Those guilty of particularly serious offences against the testator are disqualified from succeeding under the Will, §2339. Before he dies, the testator can disinherit them, §1938, and have them stripped of their compulsory portion, §§2333ff. But frequently he is no longer in the position to do so or does not discover anything of these offences during his lifetime. Therefore those who would benefit from removal of the person considered unworthy to succeed can effect the disqualification by an action for his claim to be set aside, §§2341, 2342. With the legal force of the judgement given for the claim/on account of the claim, he will no longer be eligible as an heir; anything devolving to him will be considered as having not taken place. The inheritance falls to whoever would have been appointed had the person disqualified not been alive at the time of the succession, §2344.

The disqualification of legatees and those entitled to a compulsory portion does not need to be done through a legal action but may be effected by privately contesting the eligibility of those considered unworthy, §§2345, 143.

III. The Claim for the Inheritance

395. If the inheritance initially comes into the possession of a putative heir then the real heir is entitled to claims relating to all the individual items in the estate, e.g. the claim for restitution in accordance with §985, claims arising from dispossession, §§861, 857, from unjust enrichment, §§812ff, from the proprietor-possessor relationship, §§987ff or a claim for rectification of the land register, §894.

A. *Special Claim for Restitution*

396. In addition the heir has a special overall claim for surrender of the inheritance in its entirety, the claim for the inheritance, §§2018ff. Individual and overall claims exist alongside each other; the extent of the overall claim determines the extent of the individual claims, §2029. Moreover, the law facilitates the heir's legal pursuit of the overall claim by obliging the person in possession of the inheritance to disclose information, §§2027, 2028. Procedurally, the heir can therefore take legal action against the person in possession of the inheritance in stages, §254 ZPO. In addition the overall claim can be sued for in the same way in the court having jurisdiction to decide claims against the successor, §27 ZPO, while otherwise the court with jurisdiction is determined by the location of the real estate, §24 ZPO.

B. *Subject to the Claim*

397. The claim for the inheritance can be enforced by the true heir against the person in possession of the inheritance. A single joint heir can only claim performance in favour of all joint heirs, §2039 S. 1.

The party subject to the claim is the person in possession of the estate. This is anyone who has received something from the estate on the grounds of a putative or assumed right to succeed. The claim can be directed towards a co-heir if he has assumed the status of a sole heir and with it sole possession without being entitled to do so. According to §2030 the claim is directed towards those who have received the inheritance from the person in possession of it.

In contrast, the claim cannot be directed against a third party who has single items of the estate in his possession but who does not claim any right of succession.

C. Assets to be Restituted

398. The claim contains the items that the putative heir has received and that which he has acquired by means of the inheritance (surrogation *in rem*). The use of the item and any benefits accrued must both be returned, §2020. If the return is no longer possible, then the person in possession of the inheritance must refund its value according to the laws relating to unjust enrichment, §§2021, 818 II, III. If the issue is *sub judice* or in the presence of bad faith the possessor cannot plead that the enrichment has lapsed, §§2023, 2024. In these cases the person in possession of the inheritance is liable according to §§987ff. Conversely, the person in possession of the inheritance can claim compensation for his expenses, §2022.

§2. THE CERTIFICATE OF INHERITANCE/GRANT OF PROBATE

I. The Function of the Certificate of Inheritance

399. On applying to the court of probate the heir will receive a certificate detailing his inheritance rights, §2353. This certificate provides information on the identity of the heir, the extent of the inheritance rights and likewise on arrangements for the succession of a reversionary heir or execution of the Will, §§2363, 2364. The certificate establishes a presumption of legality and completeness, §2365. Due to the irrebutable presumption of the accuracy of the certificate of inheritance it protects *bona fide* third parties who contract with those identified in the certificate, §§2366, 2367. The inheritance certificate authorizes the heir named therein to enter into legal relations, i.e. in relation to private persons, authorities and courts. For the land registry, the heir must prove his right of succession through an inheritance certificate unless the right arises from a notarial testament, §35 I GBO.

There are individual and common certificates of inheritance corresponding to the various inheritance rights, §§2353, 2357 likewise a certificate dealing only with assets in Germany which fall under foreign law of succession, §2369. If the foreign law of succession provides for splitting estates and makes part reference to German law, a certificate of inheritance according to German Law can be handed out but restricted to the domestic immovable estate.

II. Procedure for Issuance of the Certificate of Inheritance

A. Probate Court

400. The local court for the testator's last domicile has jurisdiction as the court of probate, §§72, 73 FGG. The certificate is distributed by the court clerk; it is the task of the judge if a Will is available or foreign law is to be applied, §§3 No. 2c, 16 I No. 6 RPflG.[1]

   1.   *Cf.* K. Gregor, 'Erbscheinsverfahren', JA-Referendar Skript, 1996.

B. Application

401. The certificate will only be distributed on application, for which the requirements will diverge depending on whether the succession is testamentary or intestate, §§2354ff. The court is strictly bound to the particular application; another or less comprehensive certificate cannot be issued. In those cases the court of probate will, through an interim order, grant an opportunity to make the right application.

The court of probate will investigate/examine in factual and legal respects whether the alleged right to succeed exists, §§2358 I BGB, 12 FGG. The legal right to be heard must be granted to the parties concerned, Art. 103 I GG. The certificate of inheritance will only be issued when the court is convinced of the existence of the right of succession, §2359.

C. Interim Order

402. If there is a contention between several parties concerning the right of succession, the court of probate can also make an *interim order* ('Vorbescheid'). This is an announcement, capable of being contested, that the issuance of the particular certificate is intended if no objection to it has been raised within a certain period of time. The parties can then have the legal situation clarified on appeal without it being possible for one of the parties to dispose of the estate, because the certificate has not yet been issued.

D. Withdrawal of the Certificate

403. The certificate of inheritance is evidence of the right of succession; it does not, however, form any substantively conclusive decision. If it appears that the certificate issued is incorrect (no time limit!) then the court of probate has the task of withdrawing it.[1] If it is not returned to the court then it can be declared invalid, §2361.

   1.   *Cf.* Lüke/Kerwer, 'Der zweifelhafte Erbschein', JuS 1995, 998.

E. Ordinary Proceedings with Regard to Succession Rights

404. The parties can also bring ordinary civil claims against each other for the assessment of succession rights, §256 ZPO; a judgment of this nature only has legal force between the parties and binds the court of probate to that extent when it comes to issue the certificate of inheritance.

III. The Effects of the Certificate of Inheritance

A. *Presumption of Accuracy*

405. For as long as it is in existence, the certificate has the presumption of accuracy in respect of itself, the heir, the specified right of succession and the lack of restrictions. The presumption is a rebuttable one, however, §292 ZPO. The presumption is valid until it can be proved otherwise.

B. *The Irrebutable Presumption of the Accuracy of the Certificate of Inheritance*

406. Whoever acquires an item from the person named as heir on the certificate of inheritance, confers a benefit on him or enters into another legal transaction with him with reference to the inheritance may rely on the accuracy of the certificate so long as he does not know of the inaccuracy or that the court of probate has demanded the return of the certificate on account of its inaccuracy, §§2366, 2367. Both rules fully correspond to the protection of *bona fide* rights with regard to real estate under §§892, 893.[1] The protective effect of the aforementioned rules can also be combined. For movables the certificate of inheritance has the effect of legitimation according to §2366 in connection with §§932ff; §935 is also valid here.

A priority notice protecting a claim to transfer the ownership of land ('Auflassungsvormerkung') belonging to the estate can also be attained in good faith by those who have been authorized through the certificate of inheritance.[2]

1.   *Cf.* Wiegand, 'Der öffentliche Glaube des Erbscheins', JuS 1975, 283.
2.   BGHZ 57, 341.

§3. THE HEIR'S CONSTRAINTS

I. Estates of the Provisional and Reversionary Heir

A. *Provisional and Reversionary Heir*

407. The usual heir is the final heir or the sole heir; he can dispose of the inherited estate freely. The testator can also stipulate that someone is the heir for a specific time only and after a certain point in time or emergence of a condition, another becomes heir, §2100. The provisional heir is called the 'prior heir' (Vorerbe) and the heir who follows the 'heir in reversion' (Nacherbe). Both are respective heirs of the testator, but in chronological order.

The purpose of the appointment of a reversionary heir is the maintenance of the estate as one unit and the determination of dispositions relating to the future estate.

B. Time of Reversionary Heir's Succession

408. On the reversionary heir's succession, the prior heir ceases to be the heir and the inheritance falls to the reversionary heirs, §2139. The testator can lay down a preferred point in time or with the stipulation of a condition. If only the estates of the prior and reversionary heirs are stipulated, then the reversionary heir will succeed on the death of the prior heir, §2106 I. If a person who has not yet been conceived is appointed as a reversionary heir, he will only succeed on his birth, §2106 II. Whoever is appointed as a reversionary heir is, if in doubt, also the substitute heir, §2102 I. If the testator has appointed someone to the position of prior heir without specifying the reversionary heir, then the intestate heirs are the reversionary heirs, §2104. If he has specified the reversionary heirs but not the prior heirs, then the intestate heirs are the prior heirs, §2105.

C. Legal Position of the Prior Heir

409. 1. The prior heir is the first heir to succeed and may dispose of the items belonging to the estate, §2112. In the interests of the reversionary heir there are limitations on the right of disposal of land, a ban on the disposal of land and proprietary rights likewise for dispositions for which no consideration is given, §§2113, 2114. Enforcement of judgements by personal creditors is also not permitted against the prior heir, §2115. Enforcement by creditors of the estate remains admissible.

    Whoever acquires the estate from the prior heir in good faith is protected in the same way as when acquiring from those who are not entitled, §2113 III in connection with §932 and §892 respectively.

2. The reversionary heir is protected through subrogation according to §2111: things which have been acquired by means of the inheritance belong to it. The use or enjoyment of the inheritance remains with the prior heirs for the time which they succeed to it.

3. If the time has come or the condition is realized ('Nacherbfall') the inheritance falls to the reversionary heir, §2139. The reversionary heir can demand the release of the properly administered inheritance from the prior heir, §2130. The prior heir has to compensate for possible damages, but is only liable for *diligentia quam in suis*, §§2131, 277. If the prior heir has used some of the estate in breach of his duty for his own purposes, he then must pay compensation, §2134.

4. In contrast, the prior heir can demand reimbursement for extraordinary costs for the upkeep of the property and other expenses incurred in repairing or improving it, §§2124 II, 2125. Ordinary upkeep costs and burdens are carried by the prior heir, §2124 I. Extraordinary burdens must be compensated by the prior heir, §2126.

    The prior heir's dispositions are valid after the devolution of the inheritance on to the heirs in reversion until he actually becomes aware or is held to have become aware, i.e. has constructive notice of the devolution, §2140.

D. The Legal Position of the Preliminary Heir Exempted from a Number of (Otherwise Applicable) Statutory Restrictions

410. The testator can grant the preliminary heir a greater freedom of disposition, §2136.[1] He cannot exempt the prior heir from the prohibition of dispositions without consideration, from the invalidity of enforcing judgements against him and from the principle of subrogation. The exempted heir therefore remains trustee for the reversionary heir, but may dispose of the land and does not need to compensate for possible losses. It is only the remainder of the inheritance which he has to hand over to the reversionary heir, *cf.* §§2137, 2138.

    1.   *See* J. Mayer, 'Der superbefreite Vorerbe? – Möglichkeiten und Grenzen der Befreiung des Vorerben', ZEV 2000, 1.

E. The Legal Position of the Reversionary Heir

411. On the reversionary heir's succession he becomes the heir of the testator, §2139. Before his succession the reversionary heir has an expectant right to the inheritance in accordance with the law of succession; this expectant/inchoate right is hereditary, §2108 II 1.[1]

The reversionary heir can immediately dispose of his expectant right and make use of his legal position. Creditors can also levy execution on the reversionary heir's right.

However, the reversionary heir can give up the expectant right by abandoning the inheritance through transferring his inchoate right to the prior heir, or by having disclaimed the reversionary inheritance after the first succession, §2142 I. However, the deadline for disclaiming in §1944 only begins on the reversionary heir's succession.

    1.   For the reversionary heir's claim to disclosure, *see* BGH FamRZ 1995, 158 = JuS 1995, 459.

II. The Bequest and its Testamentary Burdens

A. Bequest

412. 1. The bequest forms the basis of a claim against those charged with payment of the legacy ('Beschwerten') for release of the items bequeathed, §2174. The claim is regularly brought against the heir but can be directed against a legatee, §2147.

        Whether someone is a heir or a legatee is determined by §2087 II[1] when in doubt.

    2. The bequest can be any benefit relating to assets. If in doubt, the legacy of a specific item will be assumed to include appendages or accessories, §2164 I, but is invalid if the item does not belong to the legacy; there is no warranty against defects. An unspecified legacy ('Gattungsvermächtnis'), an alternative legacy ('Wahlvermächtnis') and a demonstrative legacy ('Verschaffungsvermächtnis') can also be bequeathed,

§2170 I. The bequest may also consist in the obligation to free any legatee from debts.

In the case of legacy of a specific item, those charged with payment of the legacy can claim compensation for expenses on devolution of the inheritance, §2185.

3. Anyone can be a legatee, even an heir, §2150. The legacy given to an heir ('Vorausvermächtnis') is differentiated from the direction given by the testator as to the partitioning of the estate in that the former can be received by the joint heir in addition to his share of the inheritance.

4. The bequest devolves along with the succession, §2176, or fulfilment of another condition, §2177. The beneficiary can accept or disclaim the legacy by declaration to the obliged person (the heir or a legatee); there is no deadline within which the repudiation must be declared, §2180.

1.   *Cf.* BayObLG FamRZ 1997, 641 = JuS 1997, 849.

B. The Testamentary Burden

413. Through a testamentary burden an obligation to perform can be imposed upon the legatee or heir without a beneficiary having a right to performance, §1940. The contents of the charge can be any act or forbearance. Frequent obligations are, for example, caring for the grave, for animals, donations for the poor, etc. Since the charge burdens the heir in a similar way to a legacy, the series of rules which are valid for the latter also apply correspondingly to the former, §2192.

If the obliged person (the heir or a legatee) simply does not observe the burden, joint heirs, heirs or others who would benefit from the cessation of the burden can demand that it be carried out; when public interest is involved, so too can the public authorities, §2194.

If the required performance is impossible, then the burden is null and void, §§2192, 2171. The bestowal in favour of the obliged person is not affected by this fact, §2195. If the execution against the obliged person is impossible because of his debts, the person who would otherwise benefit may demand release of the gift in accordance with the rules relating to unjust enrichment, §2196 I.

III. The Executor

A. *Purpose of Appointing an Executor*

414. What happens with the estate after the death of the testator in reality is a matter for the parties involved. They can share the estate by mutual agreement or practically override the arrangements of the testator. If the testator wishes to ensure that his arrangements will actually be carried out or if he wants to keep the estate as one unit until the reversionary heir succeeds to it, he can mandate an executor[1] in his Will or in a contract of inheritance, §§2197 I, 2299 I. The testator can specifically determine the executor; but he can also leave the decision to a third party or to the court of probate, §§2198, 2200. A joint heir can also be an executor.

1. *Cf.* W. Zimmermann, *Die Testamentsvollstreckung*, 2001; Bengel/Reimann, *Handbuch der Testamentsvollstreckung*, 2nd ed. 1998.

B. Types of Executors

415. The executor of the Will is the executor in charge of settlement of the estate ('Abwicklungsvollstrecker'). He has to carry out the testator's testamentary dispositions to distribute the estate among the joint heirs and to administer everything up to that point, §§2203ff.

However, the testator can also arrange an execution of the Will with long term estate maintenance ('Dauervollstreckung')[1] or an execution involving administration ('Verwaltungsvollstreckung') when, for example, he does not entrust an inexperienced sole heir with the administration of the estate or when he wishes to appoint an agent on behalf of the prior heirs, *cf.* §2209. The long term estate maintenance ('Dauervollstreckung') ends 30 years after the succession but not before the death of the heir or the executor, §2210.

The post of the executor begins after the succession and after accepting the position by declaration to the probate court, §2202. It is not commonplace for someone to be compelled to carry out the duties of an executor. The executor receives a certificate ('Testamentsvollstreckerzeugnis') on application, §2368. Its effects correspond to those of the certificate of inheritance.

The post ends on death of the executor, loss of legal capacity or where he becomes a ward of court, §2225. In addition, it ends if the executor gives notice of his intention to terminate to the probate court, §2226. It will also be terminated by a dismissal by the court of probate following an application to discharge the executor made by one of the parties on good grounds, §2227. Finally it will come to an end when all the duties have been completed.

1. *Cf.* K. Muscheler, *Die Haftungsordnung der Testamentsvollstreckung*, 1994.

C. Duties of Executor

416. The executor has to take possession of the estate and can make dispositions with respect to it, §2205, S. 1 and 2; he is not permitted to carry out dispositions which are not for consideration, §2205 S. 3. The heir cannot dispose of the individual items of the estate within the realms of the executor's competence, §2211; an acquisition by a third party in good faith is possible, however, §2211 II. The executor can incur liabilities for the legacy within the confines of proper administration, §2206.

D. Civil Proceedings with Regard to Assets

417. Assets which underpin the administration of an executor can only be made claimed by the executor, §2212; claims against the estate can not only be brought against the heir but also against the executor, §2213.[1] In order to be able to make an execution from the estate, an enforceable title (Duldungstitel) against the executor is required in any case, §2213 III.

The executor acts like an administrator in bankruptcy proceedings ('Insolvenzverwalter') according to the prevailing opinion, not as the agent of the heirs but as a party by virtue of his office ('Partei kraft Amtes') in his own name, but with economic consequences for the rights of others (called the 'Amtstheorie').

1.   *Cf.* Klingelhöffer, 'Testamentsvollstreckung und Pflichtteilsrecht', ZEV 2000, 261.

E. Position of Executor with Regard to Commercial Enterprise

418. If a commercial enterprise forms part of the estate, the execution in connection with the limited successor's liability would result in the sole trader's unlimited personal liability being undermined. Therefore according to the prevailing opinion an executor can only carry on a sole trader's business in two forms:

1.   He can carry on the business in his own name with his own unlimited liability as a trustee for the heir, or
2.   he can act as the heir's agent, the latter having to grant him the power of agency.[1]

1.   *Cf.* Ebenroth, Rdn. 687ff; Schiemann, 'Der Testamentsvollstrecker als Unternehmer', *Festschrift für Mecdicus*, 1999, p. 513.

F. Relationship Between Heir and Executor

419. The executor receives remuneration for his work, §2221. He is obliged to administer the estate properly, §2216 I. When committing culpable breaches of duty he is liable to pay compensation in accordance with §2219.

The relationship to the heir takes a form similar to that of contractual relations between principal and agent ('Auftragsverhältnis') so that the executor has a duty to disclose and a duty to hand over the estate, but also a claim for expenses. In contrast, a right to give instructions does not exist; the court of probate can only discharge the executor for a good reason on the application of one of the parties, §2227 I.

§4. THE HEIR'S LIABILITY

I. Unlimited Liability which is Capable of being Limited

420. On succession the heir immediately becomes the debtor liable for the debts of the testator, §1967 I. He has unlimited liability for these but this liability for payment out of the estate and his own assets is capable of being limited.

A. Possibilities of Limiting Liability

421. The heir has the possibility of confining his liability to the estate by order-ing its administration or by directing bankruptcy proceedings, §§1975ff. The liabil-ity is not limited by operation of law but can only be directed by the Probate or Insolvency Courts respectively on the application of the heir. If the estate is so small that the cost of the normal administration or the administration in bankruptcy of the estate are not covered, the estate must be officially set apart (Nachlassabsonderung); the heir can plead directly that there are insufficient assets in the estate i.e. *plene administravit* ('Dürftigkeitseinrede'), §1990 I, but must then surrender the estate to the creditors, §1990 I 2.

B. Loss of Possibility to Limit Liability

422. The heir loses the possibility of limiting liability in relation to all the estate creditors if he does not draw up an estate inventory within a time limit set by the court, §1994 I 2, or if he intentionally draws up this list incorrectly, *cf.* §2005 I 1. He loses his limited liability in relation to individual creditors when he makes a sworn statement ensuring the correctness of the inventory, §2006 III, or waives limited liability.

C. Public Citation of Creditors

423. In order to allow the heir to get an overview of the possible estate debts, he can request the general estate creditors to file their claims by way of a public summons (Aufgebotsverfahren) (§§946ff ZPO). Those not filing their claim on time can be excluded by a judgement of the court ('Ausschlussurteil'), §952 ZPO. The heir can refuse to satisfy creditors who have been excluded, as soon as the legacy has been depleted through satisfying creditors who have not been excluded, §1973 I 1. The heir has the same right in relation to estate creditors who only vali-date their claim five year after the succession, §1974 (called concealment 'Verschweigung').

D. Debtor of Estate's Liabilities

424. The debtor of the estate liabilities is the heir, §1967 I.

1. The heir is liable for:
    a) The debts of the testator,
    b) the debts on succession i.e. the liabilities that only arise on succession, like claims for a compulsory portion, bequests and burdens, a preferential right in respect of the matrimonial household ('Voraus') the 30 days' maintenance rule for a member of the heir's family ('Dreißigste'), the funeral costs, a demand for equalization of accrued gains ('Zugewinnausgleichsforderung')

and the duty to maintain the mother of an unborn child. The cost for the settlement and administration of the estate also belong in this category,

c) the debts of the estate heir, i.e. for the liabilities that arise from the legal acts of the heir on administering the estate.

The estate is liable for the latter, but also the heir personally, since he has incurred these debts himself. The personal liability of the heir remains in existence here, even on limiting liability.

2. If the heir continues a commercial enterprise belonging to the estate, he is liable according to §§27 I, 25 I HGB for all business liabilities of the former owner. He can exclude liability by making an entry in the register of companies, §§27 I, 25 II HGB. If he does not continue to run the firm, it remains restricted to liability purely according to the law of succession, §§27 I, 25 III HGB.

3. If the heir becomes a partner in an ordinary partnership ('OHG-Gesellschafter') on the basis of a succession clause ('Nachfolgeklausel'), he is liable according to §130 I HGB for all the earlier liabilities of the OHG without limit, in so far as he does not allow his interest to be turned into a limited partnership ('Kommanditgesellschaft') in accordance with §139 HGB or does not drop out of the company.

E. *Confinements of the Heir's Liability*

425. 1. So long as he can refuse to accept the inheritance this cannot be claimed against him, §1958. The liability will only finally eventuate when the heir has accepted the inheritance. Beforehand a creditor must apply for a provisional administrator to be nominated, §1961.

2. After the inheritance has been accepted the estate liabilities can be paid off. The three-month plea in §2014 ('Dreimonatseinrede') and the plea relating to the public invitation to assert claims ('Aufgebotseinrede') §2015 are available to the heir, however. Neither plea leads to a dismissal of a claim against the heir. Rather, he is condemned to perform his obligations subject to the limited liability, §§305 I, 782, 780 ZPO. He can then assert the limited liability by way of counter claim against the execution (§§782, 785, 767 ZPO). The pleas have no substantive effect and therefore do not exclude the heir's default.

II. Possibilities to Restrict the Liability to the Estate[1]

A. *The Administration of the Estate*

426. The heir can restrict his liability for good by ordering the administration of the estate, §1975ff.

1. The administration of the estate is directed on the application of the heir, §1981 I, if the estate is not too heavily in debt or if the heir wants to avoid the trouble of effecting the settlement and taking on the risk of his own assets being claimed.

If the heir already has unlimited liability, then he can no longer apply for the administration of the estate, §2013 I 1.

2. The administration of the estate can also be directed on the application of one of the estate creditors, if the latter has reason to believe that the heir is jeopardizing the estate creditor's claim to satisfaction, §1981 II. When the direction is made, the heir loses the right to administer and dispose of the estate, §1984. The estate and the heir's own assets become separated; the administration of the estate is transferred to the estate administrator, §1985. After the direction has been made, dispositions which have already been effected by the heir are void, §1984 I 2 BGB in connection with §§81, 82 InsO.

3. As a result of the separation of the heirs' own assets and the estate, claims between heirs and the testator remain, §1976; an estate creditor cannot offset his own claims against those pertaining to the heir; any setoff declared beforehand will become void, §1977.

4. The heir is liable like a representative for the purposes of administration before administration of the estate is directed, §1978 I 1, like an agent without authority (*negotiorum gestor* or 'Geschäftsführer ohne Auftrag') for the time before accepting the inheritance, §1978 I 2.

5. According to prevailing opinion, the estate administrator becomes active as an office-bearer in his own name; procedurally he is a party by virtue of his office. A legal relationship exists between the estate administrator and the heir ('gesetzliches Schuldverhältnis'). The administrator is liable to the heir for culpable breaches of duty, §§1985 I, 1915 I, 1833 I. He is also liable to the creditors, §1985 II.

The main task of the estate administrator is the administration of the estate and the satisfaction of the estate creditors, §1985 I. The surplus is to be handed over to the heir, §1986 I.

6 If a creditor (who has not been excluded) makes himself known after the administration of the estate has ended, then the heir can, according to prevailing opinion, refer the creditor to the remainder of the estate (corresponding to §§1992, 1990) without having to apply for the estate to be administered afresh.

  1. *See* H.-L. Graf, 'Möglichkeiten der Haftungsbeschränkung für Nachlassverbindlichkeiten', ZEV 2000, 125.

B. Proceedings on an Insolvent Estate ('Nachlassinsolvenzverfahren')

427. If the estate is heavily in debt or insolvent, the heir has to apply for the opening of estate insolvency proceedings immediately, §1980 I 1 (as amended by the EGInsO).[1]

1. Estate insolvency can be established even if the heir has not yet accepted the inheritance or has unlimited liability for estate debts, §316 I InsO. The proceedings can also begin after apportioning the estate if there are several heirs, §316 II InsO. The right to make an application is granted to any heir, to the estate

administrator ('Nachlassverwalter'), to the provisional administrator ('Nach-lasspfleger'), to the executor and to any of the estate creditors, §317 InsO. Grounds for opening proceedings are insolvency or that the estate is too heavily in debt; the heir, the estate administrator, a provisional administrator or an executor can start proceedings, even in the case of imminent insolvency, §320 InsO. The estate insolvency administrator ('Nachlassinsolvenzverwalter') must settle the estate debts and in addition convert the estate into cash. The funeral costs, the costs for obtaining a death certificate, the opening of a disposition *mortis causa*, the securing of the estate, the liabilities from provisional adminis-trators' and executors' transactions etc. are additional priority debts ('Massever-bindlichkeiten') and therefore must be settled in full, §324 InsO. Estate liabilities can also be invalidated in the proceedings, §325 InsO. Claims for the compulsory portion, bequests and burdens are only fulfilled when the other lia-bilities have been paid off, §327 InsO.

2. After the estate insolvency proceedings have come to an end the competence to make disposals is transferred to the heirs again. If the process is stayed because of lack of funds in the estate then the heir of the estate creditor can refer to the estate in accordance with §1990. If the proceedings are completed after distribu-tion the heir is only liable to the extent of the value of the estate which has been handed over to him, according to the law of unjust enrichment, §§1989, 1973 II 1. If the estate insolvency is ended by an insolvency plan, then the creditors can only claim satisfaction from the heir's own assets if the heir has unlimited liabil-ity to them or has personally committed himself to fulfill the composition quota ('Vergleichsquote') in the plan.

   1. *Cf.* Döbereiner, 'Die Nachlaßinsolvenz', in: Gottwald, *Insolvenzrechtshandbuch*, 2nd ed. 2001, p. 1531–1584.

C. *Limiting Liability when the Estate is Meagre*

428. If the estate is not sufficient to cover the costs of estate administration or estate insolvency proceedings the heir can refuse the creditor settlement without any special direction, in so far as the estate does not meet it, §1992.

§5. The Community of Heirs ('Erbengemeinschaft')

I. Joint Commitment and Joint Share in an Inheritance

A. *Estate as Common Assets*

429. On succession the estate falls in its entirety to the joint heirs, §1922 I and becomes their common assets, §2032 I. Until settlement (sharing) the heirs can only jointly dispose of the individual estate items, §2040 I. Each joint heir can only dispose of his own share of the estate, §2033 I 1.

B. Joint Ownership

430. The community of heirs is not an ownership in common ('Bruchteilge-meinschaft') but a joint ownership ('Gesamthandsgemeinschaft').[1] The estate is treated as a special fund. The community of heirs is a forced association, however, and is construed as such primarily for the purposes of liquidation. It is not an association because it lacks a common purpose. If the joint heirs continue a business belonging to the estate, an ordinary partnership does not arise by implication, rather the community of joint heirs carries the enterprise on as long as no formal transfer takes place.[2]

   1. *See* E. Sarres, *Die Erbengemeinschaft*, 1999.
   2. *Cf.* B. Dauner-Lieb, *Unternehmen in Sondervermögen*, 1998.

C. Joint Disposition on Items

431. Items of the estate may only be disposed of by all joint heirs together, §2040 I. If a individual joint heir makes a disposition, then this disposition is void if the others do not agree to it or approve it. The special assets of the community of joint heirs are legally independent; therefore a debtor cannot setoff a claim belonging to the estate with claims against the individual joint heirs, §2040 II.

D. Surrogatio in rem

432. In order to guarantee that the estate is maintained in substance, everything that has been acquired by means of the estate becomes part of it, §2041 (*surrogatio in rem*). The surrogation extends to items which have been replaced and to new acquisitions by operation of law or by means of the estate itself.

E. Disposition on Parts of Estate

433. The individual joint heir can dispose of his share of the inheritance or raise a charge on it, §2033 I 1. Dispositions made from the share of the inheritance require notary authentication, §2033 I 2. After the share is transferred the transferee is inserted into the position of the disposing joint heir in terms of rights over the assets *vis-à-vis* the administration and settling of the estate.

F. Pre-emptive Right of Co-heirs

434. Since the administration and settlement could be made more difficult by the involvement of a third party, the joint heirs have a right of pre-emption ('Vorkauf-srecht') when one of them disposes of their share, §§2034ff (but no longer after the sale).[1] The right of pre-emption only arises in the case of a sale and not on donation to a third party etc. Neither will a right of pre-emption arise on the compulsory partition by public auction ('Teilungsversteigerung') for the purpose of settlement. The right of pre-emption will also not occur if the share of the joint heir is bequeathed on his death. The right of pre-emption cannot be exercised by a single joint heir; it must be done by all of them jointly, §2035 I 1.

1.   BGH JuS 1993, 694.

II. Administration of the Estate

A. Internal Management

435. Internally the principle of joint administration ('gemeinschaftliche Verwaltung') applies, §2038 I 1.

1. According to §§2038 II 1, 745 the joint heirs can decide on conventional administration measures by a majority vote. Hence for other administration measures which are more unconventional the joint heirs must be unanimous. In cases where emergency administrative decisions must be made ('Notverwaltung') any joint heir can act alone, §2038 I 2, 2nd half sentence.

     Proper administration is determined by the nature of the estate and the interests of the joint heirs. Substantial changes to the estate do not fall within that scope and therefore require unanimity.[1]
2. There is no general duty of disclosure among the joint heirs regarding the estate; a claim for disclosure can only arise between them in single instances from a good faith requirement.[2]
3. If the joint heirs have directed individuals to become administrators, then the latter can claim reimbursement for their expenses, §670 or ask for an advance, §669. However, the joint heir must deduct the share corresponding to his own portion, §§2038 II, 748.

     The distribution of costs and burdens for the administration is determined internally in proportion to the inheritance share, §§2038 II 1, 748.
4. Likewise, the usufruct of estate property is due to the joint heirs in accordance with their shares. This is only shared out on settlement, however, §2038 II 2. If the settlement is excluded for a period longer than a year then each co-heir can claim the net proceeds at the end of the financial year, §2038 II 3.

1.   Brox, Rdn. 469.
2.   Ebenroth, Rdn. 761.

B. External Management

436. External obligations ('Verpflichtungen') must be differentiated from a disposition ('Verfügungsgeschäft').

1. As regards *obligations* everything depends on the type of administrative measure involved. If the joint heirs have made a resolution on a regular administrative

measure (unanimously or by majority vote) then the majority or one of the appointed joint heirs can represent the community of joint heirs externally.[1]

The legal transactions concluded result in rights and obligations and in estate liabilities for all the co-heirs.

For irregular administrative measures, all co-heirs must work together externally in order to act on behalf of the community of heirs.

A statutory power of agency for the community of heirs follows from §2038 I 2, 2nd half sentence for measures which derive their authority from 'Notverwaltung' i.e. measures that have to be made in emergencies. If the prerequisites for representation in emergencies are not present, then the individual acts without the power of agency. He is thus liable as a *falsus procurator* (i.e. a representative without the power of agency) §179.

2. *Dispositions* ('Verfügungsgeschäfte') can only be effected by all co-heirs jointly, §2040 I. As far as an administrative measure will lead to a disposition but can be decided upon by a majority vote or is permitted to be carried out by individuals, the disposition can also be dealt with by the majority or an individual.[2] The minority of heirs are protected sufficiently through the Surrogation principle in §2041.

3. If the estate has any claims then each joint heir can call for performance from all the heirs, §2039; the debtor can only perform for the benefit of all heirs jointly. If an individual heir asserts a claim on behalf of the joint heirs then he acts as a 'Prozessstandschafter' (i.e. a person with capacity to sue or be sued in his own name without being directly involved in the subject matter of the action). The judgment that goes either for or against the individual heir will have no legal effect for or against the other joint heirs. If all co-heirs bring an action together, they will be assuming their joint right ('Gesamthandsrecht'); they will become active as joint litigants since a decision can only be made about their collective right.[3]

1. BGHZ 56, 47.
2. Ebenroth, Rdn 765: differing view BGHZ 56, 47.
3. Ebenroth, Rdn. 768.

III. The Dissolution of the Community of Co-heirs

A. *Possibility to Dissolve*

437. The community of joint heirs is an arrangement which arises by chance and which the participants are compelled to be in ('Zwangs- und Zufallsgemeinschaft'); it should not exist any longer than necessary. Therefore in principle any joint heir can demand settlement[1] at any time, §2042 I. However, the testator can exclude settlement through his Last Will and Testament partly or in full or make it dependent upon a deadline, §2040 I, however, for no longer than 30 years after succession, §2044 II. The co-heirs do not have to carry out the settlement, rather they can simply let their community continue to exist amicably.

1. Eberl-Borges, *Die Erbauseinandersetzung*, 2000.

B. Rules for Settlement

438. On settlement the estate liabilities must be paid off, §2046; next the surplus is to be distributed to the heirs in proportion to their share of the inheritance, §2047. When apportioning the estate, the rules for an ownership in common ('Bruchteilge-meinschaft') apply, §2042 II, so that the proceeds are to be distributed in their natural state by selling and sharing them out, §§752, 753.

C. Settlement Contract

439. The actual means of settlement is not determined officially; rather, the parties involved must agree amongst themselves and conclude a settlement contract ('Auseinandersetzungsvertrag'). The court can only help by acting as an intermediary, §§86ff FGG. If the joint heirs do not come to an agreement, then one of them can make a claim for the others' assent to a settlement plan, which is established according to statutory rules.

The settlement is to be executed according to the law of property after the agreement has been concluded. In order to avoid conflicts which may arise from it, the testator can name an executor in the Will or contract of inheritance. The latter has sole responsibility for effecting the settlement, §2204 I; he is only obliged to listen to the views of the heirs in advance, §2204 II.

In addition, the testator in his Last Will and Testament can direct how the settlement is to be effected; he can also assign a third party as appears just and fair, §2048.

D. Compensation for Advancements

440. On settlement the obligation to bring into account any sum paid or settled by way of advancement ('gesetzliche Ausgleichungspflicht') must be observed, §§2050ff, likewise there is an obligation to make adjustments for special assistance or care, given to the testator during his lifetime, §2057a. These rules operate on the assumption that the descendants should inherit equal shares.

1. If one of them has received substantial advancements from the testator within the latter's lifetime, these are to be taken into account on settlement, §2050 I. The law realizes the presumed Will of the testator to this extent. On intestate succession, the testator's descendants are obliged to make payments to balance out their shares. The other intestate co-heirs are entitled to have their shares balanced out. Taken into account are advancements that a descendant has received and subsidies to income that have exceeded the normal amount, §2050 II. The same applies to expenses for education. Other donations are only to be squared if the testator, on making the bestowal or through disposition *mortis causa*, directed that they have to be set off, §2050 III.
2. The value of the shares of those joint heirs not involved in the balancing process are calculated in advance according to the estate available. Balancing the shares

('die Ausgleichung') then takes place between the joint heirs with a right to have their shares balanced ('ausgleichsberechtigte Miterben'). The value of all the donations made which are to be taken into account are added to the estate, §2055 I 2, then the value of the shares is calculated. The items each individual has to balance out must be set off against the calculated share of the inheritance, §2055 I 1. However, a duty to repay for advancements does not exist. To make equalizing easier, there is a duty of disclosure for every joint heir, §2057.

Special assistance or care, for which those involved did not receive consideration within the lifetime of the testator, is also to be included when equalizing, §2057a.

IV. The Joint Heirs' Liability for Estate Debts

A. *Liability before the Division of the Estate*

441.   1. Before dividing the estate, the estate and the personal assets of the individual heirs are strictly separated. Creditors can either access the joint assets 'Nachlass' or the personal assets of the individual joint heirs. The creditor therefore has the choice of whether to claim satisfaction from the undivided estate by means of a collective action ('Gesamthandsklage') or whether to claim from the (individual) joint heirs as joint debtors ('Gesamtschuldner'), §§2058, 421. The title certificate ('Titel') from the collective action enables the undivided estate to be seized, §747 ZPO; from the title arising from the claim against the individual heirs as joint debtors ('Gesamtschuldtitel') the creditor can claim against the individual heirs from their personal assets.

      2. Nevertheless the individual joint heir can limit his personal asset liability to his own share of the estate until the estate is divided up, §2059 I 1. This right to refuse has no substantive legal effect. It does not prevent the adjudication, and gives (by reservation in the judgement, §780 ZPO) the joint heir only the right to object to the execution by raising a specific claim ('Vollstreckungsgegenklage') (§§781, 785, 767 ZPO).

      3. The estate creditor can seize the share of the joint heir in this case, however, §2033 I BGB; §§859 II, 857 I ZPO, and force partition between the joint heirs; the other joint heirs are be seen as third party debtor in the sense of §829 III ZPO.

      4. The collective action ('Gesamthandsklage') must be directed against all joint heirs collectively; they are joint litigants by necessity ('notwendige Streitgenossen'), §62 I, Case 2 ZPO.

      5. If a joint heir is an estate creditor at the same time, then he can proceed against the other joint heirs with a claim against the joint heirs as joint and several debtors ('Gesamtschuldklage') as well as with a collective action ('Gesamthandsklage'). He must only take his own share into consideration in accordance with the obligation to bring into account sums paid in advance ('Ausgleichspflicht') when proceeding with the

claim against the joint heirs as joint and several debtors ('Gesamt-schuldklage'). The 'Gesamthandsklage' or collective action for performance from the estate does not lead to the claim being reduced. However the claim can be considered contrary to good faith in particular cases. For execution from the estate a 'Titel' will suffice against the remaining joint heirs.

B. The Heirs' Joint Liability After Division of the Estate

442. 1. After the division there are no changes in terms of the joint heirs' personal liability. Each individual is liable in addition as a joint and several debtor, §§2058, 421. What lapses, however, is the possibility of protecting his personal assets from being used to meet his liabilities (*cf.* §2059 I 1.).

2. A collective action ('Gesamthandsklage') loses its meaning after the splitting of the estate. Whether each individual heir can confine his liability to the estate depends on general rules. Administration of the estate can only be applied for while the estate is still one unit, §2062. However, estate insolvency proceedings can still take place after the estate has been divided up, §316 II InsO, which likewise will lead to liability being limited to the estate, §1975.

3. In some special cases the joint heir is not liable as a joint and several heir any longer, but as a partial debtor ('Teilschuldner'). These cases are specified in §§2060, 2061. In these cases orders can only be made against the joint heir on a *pro rata* basis. If the conditions for partial liability appear only after the court has passed judgement, then the joint heir must assert these by means of a special claim objecting to the execution ('Vollstreckungsgegenklage'), §767 ZPO.

Index

Index

Index